Food, Community, and the Spirit World

An Indian Village Study

by

Stanley Rege...

Edited and revised by
Suzanne Hanchett

Development Resources Press

D_RP

Print edition © Development Resources Press, 2022
P.O. Box 94859, Pasadena, CA 91109
www.devresbooks.com

Food, Community, and the Spirit World: An Indian Village Study/by
Stanley Regelson
Includes bibliographical references, index.

Library of Congress Control Number: 2022938303

1. Food—Customs of India. 2. Food and Social Organization. 2.
Food—Categories. 3. South Asia ethnography. 4. Karnataka—
sociology. 5. South Asia—community studies. 6. Hindu—caste
system. 7. Linguistics—food vocabulary, Kannada. 8. Hinduism—
folk customs.

ISBN 978-0-9906337-8-5 (paperback)
ISBN 978-0-9906337-4-7 (e-book)

Cover design by Rita Toews
Book formatting by Brenda van Niekerk

Cover photo: Weaver caste (Devanga) wedding, Bandipur Village,
1967

Endorsement

Stanley Regelson's *Food, Community, and the Spirit World: An Indian Village Study* lives up to its title in many significant ways, by exploring the many meanings and uses of food in different social, religious and historical contexts. Though originally published over fifty years ago, it remains a model for such studies because it presents a wide, highly detailed and linguistically sophisticated picture of the roles of food in these different contexts, based on data collected in a single village. As an illustrative example of the thoroughness of his approach, Regelson's Chapter 2, "SOME LIMITATIONS ON SOCIOCULTURAL MANIPULATION OF FOOD", considers the following types of factors which determine the availability of foods: Ecological (the cost in money and labor of foodstuffs), Seasonal (differences in availability of foods), Transport (resources available, e.g. train, bus, oxcart); Preservation Techniques (e.g. agricultural inputs, water sources); Nutritional (the effect of all these variables on the maintenance of a life-supporting diet); Distributional (the social, ecological, and religious factors which determine the availability of foods for different groups within the community); and Flavor (ways in which the taste of foods determine their acceptability in different contexts). In the following chapters, these distinctions are referred to in relevant contexts. Such detailed studies are very rare.

FRANKLIN SOUTHWORTH

Emeritus Professor of Linguistics
University of Pennsylvania
April 2022

Preface to the Second Edition

This book is a lightly edited version of Stanley Regelson's 1972 Columbia University Ph.D. dissertation, *Some Aspects of Food Behavior in a South Indian Village.* It presents an unusually thorough study of food-related language and the role of food in the social life of a rural community. Though the research was done almost 50 years ago, many of the linguistic and cultural patterns revealed in this study persist in modern rural life. In any event, the study provides a rich source of information on life in a specific time and place. Dr. Regelson was not able to finish revisions, so I have picked up where he left off.

Dr. Regelson and I lived in this Hassan District locality for almost two years in 1966 and 1967. We moved back and forth between two Brahmin villages, which we refer to as Bandipur and Chinnapura. This book emphasizes Chinnapura life but draws on insights gained in both villages. Chinnapura was located in on a peninsula formed by the joining of two rivers. The village and its surrounding area was submerged by an irrigation dam project shortly after the study was completed, forcing hundreds of families in more than 20 villages to relocate.

Other changes have also affected the life of this region and India as a whole, of course. Mysore State [Karnataka] has been re-named as Karnataka. Dalits – formerly known as "untouchables" -- no longer want to be known as "Harijans," or people of God, the term Mohandas Gandhi's followers bestowed on them. In 2017 Scheduled Caste seems to be the preferred designation. Bridewealth -- a groom's family giving money to a bride's family at a wedding -- has been largely eclipsed by ruinous demands for large dowry payments, or the bride's family giving money to the groom's.

The field of anthropology also has changed. The words "structure" and "structuralism" rarely appear in a positive light, though structuralism was a strong trend at the time of this study. Kinship is not a focus of much ethnography nowadays, although it continues to be an organizing principle of human society in all places. Voices such as those of Claude Lévi-Strauss, Louis Dumont, and others trained in the empirical and theoretical approaches of Franz Boas, British social anthropology, and the *Année Sociologique* have been drowned out by advances in "post-modern" and "post-structuralist" theory.

We are publishing this study on the assumption that detailed ethnographic observations, interviews, and other information so painstakingly collected and analyzed have a lasting value to the social sciences. The relationships of friendship and trust that result from this approach last a lifetime and produce a robust sort of information that cannot be obtained in any other way. There is ample opportunity to cross-check, to gain understanding of local consensus on many points of ethics, custom, values, and so on. We also assume that this study has some connection to possible future research on food and culture in South Asia and elsewhere. We have updated the bibliography only minimally, but a few additional works on both India and food bear directly on the content of this study, so they are included. My own book, *Coloured Rice* (1988 & 2022), resulted from the same field experience and benefited greatly from Dr. Regelson's contributions. Dr. Regelson himself went on to explore food as a part of his own Jewish way of life in a well-known article on the symbolism of the bagel. (Regelson 1981).

I wish to thank Professor Abraham Rosman for his help with this project and his enduring friendship. He was a supportive and inspiring guide to Dr. Regelson and me during our student days. And he kindly agreed to review this manuscript now, a full 50 years after we returned from our first field trip to India.

Stanley Regelson died on 3 January 2016 at the age of 84. I dedicate this book to his beloved memory.

Suzanne Hanchett, Ph.D.
Pasadena, California
September 2017

Preface to the First Edition

The anthropological field research on which this study is based was done between June 1966 and December 1967. During this period my wife and I resided in two villages, both in Hassan District, Mysore State [Karnataka]. My research was funded by a grant from the National Science Foundation, under the program of Grants for Improvement of Dissertations in the Social Sciences.

I wish to express my gratitude to the following persons who have all been most helpful to me in my research:

The people of the two villages in which we lived were extremely kind and hospitable, without exception, during our stay. My senior research assistants, Mr. A. G. George and K. Gurulingaiah, were hard-working and resourceful.

My wife, Suzanne Hanchett, has been patient and tolerant in spite of her own busy work schedule. I could not have completed this work without her.

My advisor, Dr. Conrad Arensberg, has been a kind, helpful friend and source of guidance through my years of graduate work at Columbia University.

Dr. Morton Klass and Dr. Abraham Rosman were each extremely kind in reading my work and offering excellent suggestions as well as offering the finest kind of moral support.

I am deeply indebted to Harold Conklin, who first directed my attention to the study of food behavior, and to Margaret Mead, whose helpfulness and good advice were invaluable. I would also like to express my gratitude to Robert Austerlitz, the late Uriel Weinreich, and Harvey Pitkin for their kindness. I want to acknowledge a special debt to my good friend, Owen Lynch.

Transcription of Kannada Terms

The system of transcription follows that used by MacCormack and Krishnamurti in their Kannada grammar (1966). The values of the letters employed to transcribe Kannada words are similar to those used for romanization of Devanagari script, with the following exceptions:

Vowel length is indicated by doubling rather than by a diacritic superscript. The vowel **ae** is indicated (following Kannada practice) by the sequence **ya**. Apical retroflex consonants are indicated by the use of a capital letter (**T, D, N, or L**) rather than by a diacritic subscript.

Words beginning with e- in Kannada are pronounced with an initial /y/. They therefore are transcribed as *(y)e*. Similarly, the initial o- is pronounced with a /v/ before it.

Following Nayak's (1967) observation that there is only one phonemic sibilant in spoken Kannada, I have indicated hushing sibilants only in Sanskrit words, where all are rendered **sh**. Similarly, aspirated consonants are indicated only when they are used in quotations from Brahmins, who employ them in a small number of words, usually words associated with ritual.

Certain inconsistencies in the transliteration are due to the differences between careful and rapid speech. Others are due to social dialect. I have tried to indicate these where they occur.

A number of words have traditional spellings in English; I have used these where they exist. Thus, "Kannada," "Iyengar," "Brahmin," "curry," etc. They are not italicized in such cases.

Stanley Regelson
New York, NY
1972

TABLE OF CONTENTS

TABLES AND FIGURES

Tables

Figures

ILLUSTRATIONS

<u>Maps</u>

<u>Photos</u>

House Diagrams

Chapter 1

INTRODUCTION

Indeed the circulation of food constitutes
the life's blood of caste rank.
(Marriott 1959:98)

As Marriott's comment attests, food is an important way of distinguishing castes from each other. It also is a system of classification in itself, one which is used to communicate about social relationships and personal character. The symbolic use of food in India is widespread and has a long history. As the work of Prakash (1961) and others attest, cataloguing of this fact has been of much interest to Indian writers. Details of Hindu food customs have been an important aspect of every work of ethnography dealing with India from the early nineteenth-century work of Abbé Dubois (1906) onwards.

An important account of food customs in a North Indian village is Charlotte Wiser's (1955). Wiser organizes her report as a nutritional study, rather than focusing solely on the socially meaningful aspects of food-related behavior. Anthropologists who have worked in India have addressed themselves to the question of the role of food in maintenance of the structure of "the caste system." Since the "caste system" is not a single set of relationships, but many systems of relationships in many times and places, I shall address myself primarily to the problems of one particular local system of relationships between a set of different castes, the system in which Chinnapura Village is included.

In his important 1954 article, "Status Evaluation in the Hindu Caste System," H.N.C. Stevenson brought the question of the Hindu conceptions of ritual purity and pollution clearly into an anthropological context, although, as Marriott (1959) pointed out, his was essentially a restatement of the Hindu position published repeatedly over the past two thousand years. Stevenson emphasized the fact that Hindu cultural norms rank caste occupations and foods in terms of ritual purity.

McKim Marriott referred to this as the "attributional theory" of caste ranking, and pointed out that numerous exceptions make it useless for sociological analysis. For instance, some meat-eating castes outrank vegetarian castes. He proposed an alternative, "interactional theory," which accepts the generally recognized north Indian food ranking system's raw, *pakka* (fried), *kacca* (boiled, and left-overs), and which makes possible a statistically meaningful model of caste ranking based on giving and taking various categories of foods. Observation of actual exchanges makes possible, with matrix analysis, the reporting of changes in the system of caste ranking in a village (Marriott 1968). Marriott's employment of a folk system of food types for sociological analysis is a significant descriptive contribution.

One difficulty in both of these approaches is the very concentration on bipolar interpretations such as purity *vs.* pollution, vegetarian *vs.* non-vegetarian, or high caste *vs.* low caste. If we see these as points on a complex range of distinctions rather than simple polarities, it becomes possible to introduce more facts into the discussion. Such concentration on apparent polarities has obscured the richness of the data, as Marriott (1959) points out in his critique of Stevenson.

Louis Dumont, however, points toward an approach that does seem to promise an advance in sociocultural analysis. In his detailed article, entitled "A Structural Definition of a Folk Deity," (1959) he discusses the specific isomorphy between multiple social and cultural domains in a Tamilnad community: (a) the distinctions between vegetarian deities and those who accept animal sacrifice; (b) the relation of the state to the village; and (c) the relation of the Brahmins to the non-Brahmins. Dumont offers an example of what a structural statement would involve in theoretical terms, and what he expects to be involved in terms of content:

> The general hierarchy of foodstuffs, which gives each caste's diet its hierarchical value (Blunt's "food taboo," Stevenson's "diet avoidances") is chiefly interesting for its main cleavages, which go back into history (veneration of the cow and untouchability of

beef eaters, inferiorization of a meat diet and consumption of alcohol as compared to a vegetarian diet…). But this classification of foods essentially refers back to the classification of men and to relationships between human groups, and is not a basic and independent fact resulting from a universal classification into pure and impure In detail, interpretation is not easy. ....[F]urther, there are many regional differences.... From the present point of view all this constitutes a framework of absolute criteria which the castes use to differentiate themselves hierarchically from one another: thus Brahmans probably eat meat where competition from vegetarians did not make itself felt or else where these particular Brahmans have accepted a relatively inferior position. (1970:141)

The question, "Why has Indian culture chosen to express social categories in terms of food?" may be unanswerable. But other questions are productive: "What foods have been chosen to express what social facts?" "How many different ways can food be used as a means of social expression?" "What are the categories into which foods are classified, and what is the relation of these categories to those of social classification?" I intend to address myself to some of these in this essay.

In presenting and analyzing data on food-related behavior and concepts, I shall utilize techniques of analysis which have been developed by several anthropologists over the last ten or fifteen years. Stimulated by developments in structural linguistics, Pike, Lévi-Strauss, Conklin, and Frake have been particularly influential in this field. (One historically complicating factor in this field is that the "linguistic" models used by Lévi-Strauss and Pike are no longer accepted among linguists as being above question, and so these models may eventually find themselves preserved among anthropologists while forgotten among linguists.)

Kenneth Pike (1967) justifies the use of a linguistic model for analyzing cultural phenomena in their own terms:

1) All cultural behavior is simultaneously communicative behavior, in that it is structured, traditionally transmitted, and subject to continual correction by social feedback;

2) Theoretically, language itself is a major element in the

3

cognitive processes by which cultural categories are manipulated; but minimally, we can be certain that words used by members of a culture reflect many of the categories peculiar to that culture.

It is to Pike that we owe the useful concept of "emic" and "etic" analysis. According to Pike and others, an emic analysis of language or behavior of a human group is one that uncovers the principles underlying the "native model" of reality. This is contrasted with an etic type of analysis, which uses a universally valid set of principles, and is a goal to be sought after, rather than something already achieved. (*Cf.* Lévi-Strauss 1963, Franklin 1966, and Headland, Pike, and Harris 1990)

Pike's admonition to seek out the culturally significant dimensions of contrast has led to work aimed at the discovery of emic models by a large number of anthropologists. Most of this work is directed to making it possible for the ethnographer, "to state rules of culturally appropriate behavior." (Frake 1964:133)

In the work of Conklin, however, we find suggestions that the purpose of this type of ethnography is not only the setting up of properly described domains with the intention of learning rules of behavior concerning elements of the domain, but also the comparison between the structuring of domains within a culture in an attempt to recognize isomorphies between different areas of behavior. (Cf. Conklin 1955)

One technique associated with the names of Conklin and Frake is the method of "componential analysis" of meaning, an attempt to define the relation of words in a particular domain of meaning by discovering the minimum semantic components (similar to "distinctive features" in linguistic analysis) that create contrast and hierarchy among them. This is one method of arriving at ordered linguistic sets; it is clear, however, that sets involving behavior other than linguistic behavior are also important.

The proponents of this type of analysis have pointed out that the method assumes a prior knowledge of what the basic units of the system are. Without a decision on the nature of these units, such analysis is impossible. Unless informants provide hints themselves, one cannot make this decision directly from word lists.

In reference to the problem of comparison between different cultural domains, and the determination of isomorphies among domains, Lévi-Strauss states this as a goal more clearly than Conklin does, in his writing on the structure of cooking methods:

> After elaborating our diagram so as to integrate all the characteristics of a given culinary system (and no doubt there are other factors of a diachronic rather than a synchronic nature: those concerning the order, the presentation and the gestures of a meal), it will be necessary to seek the most economical manner of orientating it as a grille, so that it can be superposed on other contrasts of a sociological, economic, aesthetic or religious nature: men and women, family and society, village and bush, economy and prodigality, nobility and commonalty, sacred and profane, *etc.* **Thus we can hope to discover for each specific case how the cooking of a society is a language in which it unconsciously translates its structure--or else resigns itself, still unconsciously, to revealing its contradictions.**(Lévi-Strauss 1966a:940, emphasis added)

In *Structural Anthropology* (1963a:86) Lévi-Strauss proposes the application of a linguistic model to the facts of cuisine. He introduces the example as if it had been chosen at random, and so disclaims responsibility as to whether the scheme will actually produce fresh insights or not. Lévi-Strauss uses the binary plus or-minus mode associated with the distinctive feature theory of the Prague School of linguistics. His distinctive features are meant to be universal in application. (The possibility of devising such a set of features is as controversial in linguistics - see Chomsky and Hall, 1968 - as it is in gustology, to follow the example from gusteme.)

In his later paper on food ("The Culinary Triangle," 1966a), and in the title of the first volume of his trilogy on myth (*The Raw and the Cooked,* 1969), Lévi-Strauss revealed that his seemingly "chance" use of a gustological example was not chance at all, but an enduring interest. In "The Culinary Triangle," he moves up from the distinctive-feature mode of analysis to a phonemic level, assuming the existence of the "consonant triangle" *p-t-k* as a universal component of natural languages. A gustological triangle is then posited to match it, of raw-cooked-rotted. (We will return to this discussion in the Conclusion.)

Unlike Conklin and Pike, Lévi-Strauss is working on the assumption that certain isomorphies between different fields of behavior are due to basic patterns in human nature. The American scholars prefer to speak of seeking the patterns that repeat themselves within a particular society. Their position seems to be more pragmatic, and thus more in line with the American empirical tradition in anthropology, to seek explanations after finding that certain patterns of isomorphy are widely distributed. Are they due to ecology, demography, limited possibilities, human physiology, or Upper Paleolithic inventions so effective that they survive to modern times?

The isomorphy between structures of different semantic domains is what makes it possible for an element in one domain to symbolically represent an element in another field. We are dealing then with symbolism by means of structure, a very specific concept, rather than the structure of symbolism, an exercise impossible to verify.

For instance, a Brahmin village of the type in which I did my research is divided into three parts: the *kooTe*, where the Brahmins live; the *peeTe*, where the non-Brahmins live; and the A.K. Colony, where the Harijans [Scheduled Castes/Dalits] live. An ordinary house is divided into three areas; the kitchen, reserved for the family; the outer rooms; and the verandah. We are not surprised, on the basis of isomorphy between the village structure and the house structure, to learn that a visiting Harijan is allowed only as far as the verandah.

We will deal with a number of ways of describing foods that are characteristic of the society. Some of them point clearly to patterns of daily use, cultivation, and marketing. Some of them point to more esoteric patterns. The number of easy generalizations is small, and the most striking patterns can be brought to the level of universals only by rather tenuous hypotheses, which will nevertheless be explored.

As I will try to show, the effect of such repeated patterns is that suggested by Lévi-Strauss in *The Savage Mind* (1966b:68):

>...[T]his network of systems will react to any change affecting one of its parts like a motor with a feedback device: governed...

by its previous harmony, it will direct the discordant mechanism towards an equilibrium which will be at any rate a compromise between the old state of affairs and the confusion brought in from the outside.

Before setting forth a number of models deriving from the data, it is necessary first to identify the structural units and the social setting of Chinnapura; to identify the food items used; to establish the association between social structure and food behavior; and to explain some of the broader rules of behavior, in relation to food. It is also necessary to bring in certain elements of the larger Hindu context, where certain significant themes are in play. By covering these topics in the following chapters, I shall attempt to describe the components of the system of socio-cultural distinctions. In the final chapters I shall discuss structural implications of these phenomena.

The reader can see by now, that the present study gives little attention to nutrition, as important as this is to all groups concerned. I am not qualified to do a nutritional study, beyond noting some obvious differences in quality and quantity of foods consumed by families of different socio-economic status groups. The focus here is on food behavior and food-related language as a symbolizing and structuring aspect of rural life and relationships.

Chapter 2

SOME LIMITATIONS ON SOCIO-CULTURAL MANIPULATION OF FOOD

A central requirement of any symbol system is the lack of predictable connection between the referent and its symbolic representation. Linguists refer to this as "arbitrariness" (Hockett 1960:90). The meaning of any particular word, for example, is in no way determined by the sounds that comprise it.

Arbitrariness is not the same as complete freedom. In the case of spoken language, the sounds that may be used are confined to those which the human vocal apparatus can produce. Further, since speech is produced using organs whose prime functions are alimentary and respiratory, the activities associated with its production must be such that the speaker neither suffocates nor starves. Because of the arbitrary connection between sound and symbol, the study of language is not a branch of otolaryngology.

Similarly, food behavior, viewed as a symbolic and communicative system, is separate from the nutritional and ecological basis on which it rests. Linguistics can ignore most otolaryngological facts because human anatomy is invariant throughout the species, and all human speech must operate with it in essentially the same way. "Phonetics," the study of all possible speech sounds, is constrained by anatomy.

The geographical and technological facts that create the ecological basis for food behavior, on the other hand, are not universal. The codified uses of food by different cultures differ widely. We do not yet know if there is a universal ("etic") set of food categories, symbols, and practices equivalent to the minimal set of sounds that combine and recombine in human languages.

It is clear that, if the utilitarian aspects were the only factors determining the importance that a culture attaches to foods, we could hardly talk of food symbolism. In Chinnapura, as in other human communities, choices of customary foods for special occasions have no obvious survival or practical basis.

Nonetheless, food – being essential to life, along with water -- is a utilitarian good even when it is operating as a symbol. The limitations constraining its symbolic uses are not always obvious. Many types of limiting conditions were evident in Chinnapura Village. It is far from paved roads, for example, and it is characterized by dependence on local subsistence agriculture. It therefore is especially affected by the following types of limitations:

Ecological. With few exceptions, the foods consumed in the area are grown within thirty kilometers, one full day's oxcart journey. Therefore, foods that cannot be grown in the local climatic and soil conditions are rare. Goods brought in from outside were those whose value was very great in proportion to their size and weight, such as cinnamon and cloves, or coffee from neighboring districts.

Seasonal. Certain foods are scarce or unavailable at certain times of the year, plentiful at others. When an item is in season, it will probably be eaten every day. When we first arrived, during the cucumber season, we were under the impression that curried cucumbers were daily fare throughout the year. Fortunately, this impression was soon proved wrong.

Transportation. Naturally, if more effective transportation techniques had been available in Chinnapura, the territorial ecological base would have been quite different. But the bullock cart is still the chief method of transporting produce in this region.

Preservation Techniques. Many crops involve complex irrigation and crop rotation systems. Furthermore, changes in agricultural practices were being made at the time we were there. These included the use of insecticides, of chemical fertilizer, of electrically powered tube wells, and the introduction of fast-growing, high-yield hybrid rice. Alternatively, milk production was held down by the fact that cattle were bred as draft animals rather than for milk. (It should be pointed out that except for the tube wells, the changes in agricultural technology probably have implications for the biochemical character of the foods produced.)

Nutritional. This aspect, of course, includes what we think of as the central question in dealing with food. For the purpose of this discussion, we must presume that a minimal life-supporting diet can be defined. We must presume further that a traditional diet, one eaten over a large area over a long period of time, will have developed in such a way that these minimal requirements will be met in enough people so that the population survives as a group. Thus we are not surprised to find that the amino acid content of the rice/red gram combination and of the finger millet/horse gram combination compares reasonably well with the amino acid content of whole proteins.

Distributional. In a hierarchically organized social system, where it is conceivable for one class to skim off most of the resources, it is likely that some system will develop to guarantee some degree of nutrition among the less favored social groups. One example of this would seem to be associated with the protein sources of the three main classes in Chinnapura. Even poor Brahmins have a certain amount of milk available. Non-Brahmins, even dairymen, sell most of their milk to Brahmins. However, they are permitted goat and other meats, which are not permitted by custom to Brahmins. Harijans have little opportunity to get either milk or goat meat; but beef, at a cost of about one-tenth that of goat meat, often is available to them. The Brahmins are not in a position to raise the price of meat by increasing demand for it; nor can the non-Brahmins affect the market in beef.

The South Indian system of caste-based food taboos is reminiscent of a taboo on organ meats among white people in America. The United States is the only western country that has a very strong taboo against the eating of organ meats. In our caste-like system this taboo assures that people of the African American minority, who do not share this repulsion for organ meats, will be provided with some high protein food. Yet this system does not involve the elaborate symbolic support that is characteristic of the Hindu caste system.

Flavor. Cooking and preparation of food is a cultural universal. It involves complex biochemical combination and processing; in fact, it is the model on which all modern chemistry rests. In this ritual, furthermore, system flavors are named and symbolically manipulated.

Cooking to make food palatable usually requires the full-time services of some adult members of the population. It is doubtful that this would be necessary if the science of nutrition were as simple as we pretend to think it is. If all that is involved is "mere flavor," then we are observing a terrible waste of human resources. It is more logical to doubt the applicability of the word "mere."

It seems possible that the different spices and techniques involved in food preparation produce biochemical combinations that may be needed by people whose diets have certain gross characteristics, whose daily behavior is of a certain type, and perhaps whose personalities require biochemical modification to be ideally suited for the social structure. As Moody (1965) has suggested, for example, the known effects of poppy seeds on blood pressure may have implications for psychological states. The use of coffee and betel nut certainly do.

Not very much is known about the subtler trace biochemicals in food, nor of their effects on physiology. It is the scientist's duty to search for explanations. Rather than shrugging off the facts that a South Indian mother tends to give her son a chili pepper and an American mother tends to give her son a sweet, as mere "customs," we should attempt to explain such differences in taste.

More investigations of foods should be applied to the extraordinarily sensitive biochemical metering system that is the human palate, and the physiological and psychological effects of the biochemicals involved in specific cuisines.

Another type of explanation for taste takes nutritional requirements into consideration, but only in a superficial way. For example, the interest in spicy foods in India has been explained by reference to the fact that chili peppers contain Vitamin C. However, peppercorns alone served the same culinary purpose until 100 years ago, when chili peppers were first introduced into the Indian cuisine from the New World; and peppercorns do not contain Vitamin C.

These minimal conditions leave room for an enormous social and cultural variety in treatment of foods. Symbolic uses of food operate within a sociocultural context. For instance, the left-hand/right-hand division is part of a global scheme in the Hindu world outlook of general right-left distinctions. Another example is the three-part division of society, into Brahmin/non-Brahmin/Harijan sections. Such sociocultural concepts and organizing devices are reinforced and reflected in types of foods eaten by the different classes and the many forms of ritualized food preparation associated with rites of passage and other occasions.

Chapter 3

THE SOUTH INDIAN SETTING: CHINNAPURA VILLAGE

Chinnapura (*cinnaapuura*) was a village of 90 households in Hassan District, Mysore State [Karnataka] [now renamed as Karnataka]. It was situated on a peninsula within the confluence of the Hemavati and Yagachi Rivers. The Hemavati flows on to Madras, where it is tributary to the Cauvery. Maps 1 – 4 show Mysore, Karnataka, Hassan District, and the locations of our study villages.

I lived with my wife in this village for approximately eight months, between June and December, 1967. We set up housekeeping in Chinnapura, together with our assistants, Mr. A.G. George, Mrs. Joyce George, and K. Gurulingaiah, after living across the river for about a year in a nearby village, which we call Bandipur. Both Chinnapura and Bandipur are pseudonyms.

Shortly after we finished our ethnographic studies and left India, Chinnapura and its neighboring villages were evacuated, and the whole peninsula was flooded. A dam project had turned the whole area into a huge reservoir to support irrigation in the wider region. The only sign of its former life was a small "island" in the middle of the reservoir formed by the tip of a village temple. [*Editor's Note:* This book is written in the present tense, but the village is no more.] Photos of village people and their life are attached at the end of this book.

The Village and Its Sections

Chinnapura is a Brahmin village. This means chiefly that it contains a large settlement of Brahmins. (The term "Brahmin village" is discussed in Gough, 1960. Her Tanjore village has much in common with Chinnapura.) Chinnapura and two nearby hamlets comprise a *jooDi*. This formerly was a tiny principality granted by the Maharaja of Mysore, exempt from taxes, not subject to outside interference, and technically the property of the *jooDidaar* and his descendants. The present *jooDidaars* are the last ones, since land reform after Indian Independence abolished such grants.

The village is divided into three sections, each occupied by a different type of caste grouping: Brahmins, "non-Brahmins," and Harijans (also called Adi Karnataka, or A.K.'s, now known as Scheduled Castes or Dalits). Large land holdings have been in the hands of the Brahmins. The non-Brahmin group includes small land holders, tenant farmers, artisans, and merchants of eight different castes (*jaatis*). Harijans' chief income is from agricultural day-labor. Like most villages of this type, Chinnapura's three sections are called *kooTe*, "fort" (the Brahmin neighborhood); *peeTe*, or "market" (the non-Brahmin neighborhood); and the "A.K. Colony" (*ee ke kaalani*), a Harijan hamlet. All the people of Chinnapura are Hindus.

Chinnapura Brahmins are of two *jaatis*: Smartha (*smaarta*), who are Shaivite Kannada speakers; and Iyengars (*ayyangaar*), Srivaishnavas who speak a dialect of Tamil among themselves. A Sanskrit word for the Brahmin section, occasionally used by Brahmins, is *agarahaara*. Along with the houses of the two major groups of Brahmins, the *kooTe* contains the houses of a handful of government workers, some non-Brahmins of the so-called service castes (*i.e.*, Washermen and Barbers, essential to ritual purity), and an immigrant Marathi tailor. The *kooTe* contains a large temple of the god Narasimhasvaami (Vishnu's lion avatar). The priest is an Iyengar.

The word *kooTe,* "fort," refers to the fact that this was an old walled village. some of the wall still stands. It is a reminder of the wars of the Palegars (*paalegaara*), petty robber barons who dominated the area until the start of the nineteenth century. The *jooDidaars*, Brahmin brothers who own most of the village land, live in a large house just outside the old village fort wall. Their house is divided into two parts. The brothers have not spoken to each other in decades.

The *peeTe,* or "market" section contains the houses of the rest of the non-Harijan villagers. It also has a small shop, selling groceries and sundries, and a flour mill. The shop and mill are owned by Brahmins. The *peeTe* faces onto an open square near the village gate. The gate is marked by a pipal tree (*Ficus indica;* Kannada, *aaraLi mara*), and a neem tree (*beevin mara*). There is a pipal tree at the entrance to most villages. In fact, in a lower caste dialect, the word for the tree is *haLLi mara,* meaning "village tree." To one side of the square is the temple of the goddess Maramma. Maramma, who is said to accept animal sacrifices, is serviced by priests of the Washerman caste, who rotate priestly responsibility among multiple lineages (clans).

Like those of most nearby villages, the Chinnapura *peeTe* is subdivided into rows of houses (*biidi*, "street") where individual castes tend to cluster. Growth and shrinking of caste populations combine with sale and exchange of house sites, however, to keep streets from being completely homogeneous. However, few are as much of a hodgepodge as Chinnapura's *peeTe*, which even contains a Brahmin household. Outsiders sometimes comment on the disorder disapprovingly.

The name of the Harijan hamlet, *ee ke kaalani,* is in fact English: "A.K. colony." A.K. stands for *aadi karNaaTaka* ("original inhabitants of the Kannada land"). The latter term was introduced to replace *Holeeru* (or *Holeeya*), the group's traditional name. A second group of Harijans, traditional leather workers, *ee di* (A.D., *aadi draavida,* "original Dravidians") or *MaaDigaru*, are not represented in this particular village. "Harijan" itself, meaning "people of God," is a term coined to replace the entirely negative "untouchable." This or A.K. were the polite terms used by others during the time of our fieldwork. [*Editor's note:* Dalit, the term devised by Dr. Ambedkar, is presently considered the most respectful designation for this category of castes throughout India. Scheduled Caste is also considered a suitable designation by members of this community.]

A.K. colonies of this region usually are small clusters of houses outside the marked village boundary. Chinnapura's is a separate, nucleated hamlet, about an eighth of a mile outside the village by way of the village gate. However, it is only twenty yards from the Brahmin houses if one cuts across the fields. The A.K. colony has its own access to the riverfront, downstream from the area used by other castes.

The Peninsula with 28 Villages

The peninsula where Chinnapura is located is surrounded on three sides by water. Forested hills form a barrier on the mainland side. This peninsula is about 12 square miles in size and contains twenty-seven other villages and hamlets besides Chinnapura. (See Maps 4a and 4b.) Some of the twenty-eight villages have names but are in fact empty sites. Twenty-eight is a number that turns up frequently in story-telling and conjuring. And it would not be surprising if there never were actually twenty-eight villages at any particular time. An annual festival involving all "twenty-eight" villages occurs in a meadow near Chinnapura. There is a *naaD pancaayat*, or regional council, for the 28 villages, composed of their headmen. It is still the ultimate arbiter in serious disputes. There are, in addition, two government-sponsored panchayats: one in Chinnapura and one in another village. Each is assigned fourteen villages. The government panchayats deal mostly with irrigation works and government-funded development projects, although they sometimes arbitrate disputes as well. Chinnapura is the only village of the twenty-eight that has a clinic, a mill, and a government middle school. Only one other village has a shop. Each village has a *patel*, or headman, a hereditary office. The *patel* is expected to record marriages and to provide other vital statistic to the government.

The area is rather thinly populated compared to the land outside the rivers, and the peninsula villages are considerably smaller. A great deal of the peninsula is government-owned forest and meadow land, which supplies wood for fuel and the manufacture of charcoal, as well as grass for common livestock-grazing.

Although the rivers are usually easy to traverse by foot, and the hills are not at all impenetrable, the peninsula villages are more closely connected with each other than with the outside world. About half of all marriages reportedly take place within the area. The isolation is augmented by a road system that seems not to have been improved since the nineteenth century. The area has been systematically undeveloped by the government because it is scheduled to be submerged by a dam backwater.

Land and Livelihoods

Chinnapura has several irrigation tanks that make extensive paddy cultivation possible. The staple grain, however, is finger millet (*raagi*), which grows on "dry," or unirrigated land (*hola*). Chinnapura is at the edge of the Malnad, the rainy high plateau of western Mysore State [Karnataka]. A fertile red loam is the typical soil. The region did not suffer as severely from the droughts of the 1960s as the lands across the rivers.

Various grams and pulses, along with mustard and other seasoning foods, are grown between the rows of *raagi* and on the land during the off-season. There is only one grain crop a year in this area, due to the seasonal availability of water.

There is a great deal of fishing in the rivers -- by local individuals, by organized parties, and by itinerant professionals. Rabbit and field-rat hunting parties also are formed, providing important protein sources for most non-vegetarians.

During the greater part of the year, it is possible to walk across the Hemavati River in waist-deep water. But during the rainy season a leather boat carries commuters from one side to the other. Chinnapura's post office is a subsidiary of Bandipur's, our larger village outside the river junction. The postman comes daily carrying bells and a spear, since the lands between the two villages are defined by the government as "jungle." Oxcarts move across the river. They are the principal means of land transport for most peasants. Ox buying and selling is a major preoccupation, a subject of discussion as enthralling to people here as cars are to Americans. Oxen are treated with the greatest care, more carefully tended than are cows.

The relatively low population density of the peninsula makes possible a great reliance on wild game and plants. Until recently big game, including tigers, were common. In our own time, two of the 28 villages reportedly were attacked by wild elephants, though we did not see them ourselves.

Coconuts, areca, and sugar cane are among the cash crops grown in the area. Sandalwood trees abound, but they are technically all government property. There is a black market in the fragrantly scented wood. In November 1967 the state of Mysore abolished prohibition, but while we were present in Chinnapura, bootlegging was an important village industry.

A weekly market is held on Saturdays in Bandipur. Villagers buy and sell produce there. Some also travel 17 miles to the town of Hassan, to sell butter and other produce and to Magge, a village eight miles away.

Religious Specialists

Religious activity is all-pervasive. Frequent festivals, special offerings to gods and ancestors, and rites of passage command significant amounts of villagers' time. The proliferation of religious specialists is striking. The Brahmins regard themselves as the only proper priests and perform weddings for all other Hindus except Harijans. It also is possible, however, for the oldest male of a bride's family to assume the priestly function at marriages. Although Brahmins often perform weddings for non-Brahmins, they confide that a non-Brahmin marriage is not a real sacrament, since only *slokas* (verses) are chanted, and not *mantras* (spells). A Brahmin must change his sacred thread after performing a wedding for any caste considered lower than the Peasants. And he therefore may refuse to participate in such weddings because of the effort involved.

A temple of Maramma is serviced by Washerman priests; a river goddess temple, by a Fisherman; and a Siva-of-the-Confluence temple, by Lingayats. Lingayats are a religious sect devoted to the god Siva. The religious group is in some ways organized parallel to the Hindu caste system, and separate from it. (See MacCormack, 1953) In the Chinnapura area, where Lingayats are a minority, they are simply treated as another non-Brahmin *jaati* (as are Muslims, visiting Americans, Jains, etc.).

A non-Brahmin priestly caste group known as *aynoru* has both Vaishnava and Saiva subcastes, who service a number of temples as well as being specialists in *shaanti kelsa* (literally, "peace making") -- *i.e.*, the work of putting the departed at peace, required at non-Brahmin funerals. Some of the members of this group are vegetarian, and some are not. All the *aynoru* men affect a style of dress similar to the Brahmins, but most acknowledge their own non-Brahmin status. The *aynoru* women are distinguished by the sari being draped over the right shoulder instead of the left. Unlike the Brahmins, who pray in Sanskrit, their liturgy is entirely in Kannada.

Every non-Brahmin Hindu caste has lines of initiates called *daasaru* (literally, "slaves," meaning slaves of God) who are needed for certain religious functions. Little of this has been reported by ethnographers, because the Brahmins, who influence much of the writing on religion, see it as a form of disorganized heathenism. The *daasaru* are members of specific lineages in Vaisnava subcastes of most non-Brahmin *jaatis*. they are connected with the cult of the god at Tirupati, a pilgrimage center in Andhra State [now Telangana]. The god is variously known as Venkateshvara, Srinivaas, Venkataraama, and Timma. Tirupati's god is in one sense the national god of South India.

TABLE 1. Chinnapura Population (1967)

Castes (*jaati* name) & Caste Groups	No. HH	Population	Mean HH Size
Brahmin (Smartha & Iyengar)	22	113	5.65
Non-Brahmins			
Smith (Achari)	2	11	5.5
Barber (Agasa)	4	15	3.75
Fisherman (Bestaru)	2	6	3.0
Washerman (Dhobi)	12	53	4.42
Peasant (Okkaliga)	16	70	5.0
Marathi Tailor	1	4	
Lingayat	2	2	
Scheduled Caste/A.K. (Holeya)	29	127	4.54
Total	90	401	4.72

Village Social Structure: Caste, Subcaste, Kinship, and Class

The parameters of the social system are caste (*jaati*), kinship and residence, and class. To non-Indian eyes caste is the most visible, although each of the others is an important organizing principle in the society. Table 1 presents the results of our village census, counting households caste-wise. As this list shows, most castes in this region, as elsewhere in India, have a traditional, hereditary occupation.

The classical Indian scheme of four caste categories, or *varNas* (Brahmin "priests," Kshatriya "warriors," Vaisya "merchants," and Shudra "peasants/laborers"), is not much used in common parlance of this area, although educated Brahmins refer to it now and then. The three-part division of caste levels -- Brahmin, non-Brahmin, and Harijan -- is the over-arching social framework throughout the region.

In Hassan District, Brahmins are about five percent of the population, Harijans are about fifteen percent, and the rest are non-Brahmins or people of other religious and ethnic groups. The twenty-eight villages each have different caste compositions. One contains only

Shepherds; another, Muslims and Peasants; another, only merchants, Lingayats of priestly lineage, and Harijans.

Chinnapura has a relatively broad range of castes, compared to other villages. The type of caste distribution of Chinnapura is typical of Brahmin villages of South India. (Beteille, 1965; Srinivas, 1955; Gough, 1960; Sivertsen, 1963.) Chinnapura is the *de facto* peninsular capital.

The members of every caste are highly aware of status rank and other differences between themselves and members of other castes. The extremes to which this is carried are perhaps the most striking fact about social life in India. Castes are "endogamous" groups, meaning that marriage is socially acceptable only with people of the same caste, and perhaps only the same subcaste.

The tendency to fragment social groupings is extreme. Beyond caste and subcaste divisions, it is carried to the point where individual lineages or houses may separate themselves permanently from ordinary relations even with their caste-mates. (These breaks seldom cross village boundaries, however, and both groups usually continue normal relations with caste-mates outside of the village. Within a village, however, these separations may last even after their origins (typically inheritance disputes) are forgotten.

Most castes are divided into subcastes. The word "subcaste" has been used with two different meanings. The first is the case of actually separate castes who happen to follow the same traditional occupation. One example of this is the two "subcastes" of Fishermen. The *gange mata* are professional itinerant Fishermen whose home language is a Marathi dialect. (The names of the two castes reflect the names of two wives of Siva.) The *gauri mata* are settled Kannada speakers.

Another example is the Smartha and Iyengar Brahmin "subcaste" distinction. The Smarthas of this region are Kannada-speaking Shaivites; the Iyengars are, as I have said above, Tamil-speaking Srivaishnavas. There is no legitimate marriage or inter-dining between the two groups. This definition of "subcaste" is not the one that is used in this book.

According to the definition we will follow, a caste is divided into theoretically endogamous subcastes by a small number of ritual or customary differences, but members of these different subcastes all consider themselves to be members of the same caste. It is common to say that marriage should not take place between members of different subcastes, and many informants will flatly deny that it does. It seems, however, that a limited amount of intermarriage regularly occurs without disapproval. Even when an informant admits that inter-marriage takes place, he will often say that men of his own subcaste may marry women of the other subcaste, but that his group will not give women to the other. This reflects the traditional view that wife-takers are superior to wife-givers and places his own subcaste in a superior position. In some cases this will be a true description of marital exchange among the groups. In other cases members of both subcastes will claim that they take brides from the other subcaste, but will not give women in marriage to them. In these cases investigation usually reveals that both types of exchange take place.

Within a subcaste members may be divided into *deevara okkalu*, *i.e.*, groups with the same house god (*mane deevaru*). This is a subtle structural difference, sometimes giving the appearance of a subcaste. For instance, Chinnapura has one family of Saivite *daas* Peasants who occasionally speak of themselves as a separate *jaati*. This contrasts with other castes, among whom very little attention was paid to subcaste differences, although customary rituals of the different *vokkalu* may differ somewhat.

There is a rivalry of sorts between the two Brahmin *jaati*s. Smarthas claim that the founder of the Iyengar Srivaishnava sect conferred Brahmin status on "Shudras" in order to expand his ranks. (The word Shudra is a pejorative when spoken by a Brahmin.) The Iyengars, for their part, have no doubt of their own superiority to Smarthas. This rivalry, however, is being modified in favor of a tendency to recognize each other as fellow Brahmins. Ceremonies may be performed together; formerly, they were not. Except for the temple priest, whose wife's fecundity and whose ritual duties have kept him from properly supervising his land, all the Brahmins of Chinnapura could be considered wealthy. The Brahmins are all committed to the maximum education for their children. Except for the unemployables, almost all of those in their twenties and thirties live in the cities and come home only for holidays.

The Smiths are heavily Sanskritized vegetarians, but are nevertheless considered to be very low status by most other non-Brahmins, who will not take food from them. They make jewelry, buy it and sell it. They also may do blacksmith work on agricultural implements and some carpentry.

The Washermen, Fishermen, and Barbers are nearly all very poor. Their traditional *jajmani* duties to other castes still bind them, although they also do work for cash.[1]

The word "Peasant" will be used throughout this essay to refer to the caste known as Okkaliga or Gowdas (*gauDoru*). They are the numerical majority throughout Mysore State [Karnataka]. Their traditional specialty, above and beyond farming, is cattle and milk production. They are proud of their meat-eating, their moustaches, and their hair-trigger tempers. These martial characteristics give them a sense of superiority to the Brahmins, whom they consider sissified weaklings. Nevertheless, they accept the facts of Brahmin economic and religious dominance.

There are two Peasant subcastes in the area: *daasa* ("slaves" of God) and *muula* ("original"). The *daas(v)okkaligas* are characteristically Vaishnavas, the *muul(v)okkaligas* Saivas. Certain distinctions in the consumption of meat are also observed. (See Chapter 5.)

The Peasants and the Brahmins for some years have each considered themselves to be the most important caste in the wider region. The caste system combined with the universal vote has resulted in heavy representation of Peasants in the various political bodies. The Brahmins, however, through superior education and judicious spending of money, are still holding their own. It was widely assumed that political conflicts between these two groups would be a major problem in Mysore State [Karnataka] after Indian Independence. As it turned out, however, political conflict has been blunted by the establishment of linguistic states. The Kannada-speaking area of northern Mysore that was annexed from the old Bombay Presidency is overwhelmingly Lingayat. Lingayats

---

[1] The *jajmani* system is an arrangement between castes, in which each group regularly provides services to others according to its traditional occupation in exchange for foods, grains, and/or certain types of gifts.

are now the majority in the new state, and they are more politically influential than either the Peasants or the Brahmins alone.

It should be remembered that under a line of socially responsible maharajahs Mysore had been a "model state" of princely India. Roads, schools, and government services were high above the all-India level. North Karnataka, as it was known before being annexed to Mysore, was a neglected and underdeveloped area under British rule. The present government is spending heavily on bringing the north up to the southern level. This investment is bitterly resented by many residents of the old princely state.

The Brahmins of Mysore are usually found in riverside villages. They claim it is because a year-round supply of water is necessary for their ritual ablutions. The non-Brahmins say that Brahmins simply own all the richest, river-watered land, and that Brahmin wealth is due to the patronage of the Maharajah. This is partly true. Endowing Brahmins was considered an act of great spiritual merit. It is clear, however, that much of their wealth is due to money lending and to other sharp practices that literate people can work on the illiterate. Brahmin women are never seen in the heavy cloth "snuff-colored" (dark reddish pink) saris worn by non-Brahmin and Harijan women. Many of them wear silk saris daily.

Traditional and New Forms of Patron-Client Relationship

Alongside mandatory *jajmani* system of service relationships between castes – and increasingly more important than it -- exist the wage-labor system and the market economy, in which people play the roles of employer-employee or buyer and seller. Certain personal obligations may become associated with employment, as they are with *jajmaani* relationships. In cases of long-term employment of a family servant, for example, an employer is often expected to pay the employee's wedding, initiation, or health expenses. He is also expected to deal fairly with his daily laborers. The character of such a man is often judged by the grace and generosity with which he meets these obligations. He is measured on a scale of "respect" (*mariyaadi*), which has moral and even economic implications. If one's respect is low, he will find himself subjected to swindles, deceit, and lack of support in conflicts. If he acts in accordance with the moral demands of his position, however, he may become a "big man" (*doDDaavaru*), or patron, with many supporters to do his bidding.

Kinship, Gender , and the Hindu Home

Relations between kin are defined in the Kannada language (and the Dravidian kinship system generally) and in practice by four principles. These are: (1) generation, (2) relative age, (3) patrilineality, and (4) sex. Behavior follows linguistic categories closely, though with some discrepancies. Family leadership, for instance, goes to the eldest brother on the father's death; but land is parceled out equally among brothers, if and when the joint family separates its holdings.

Extreme respect is expected from a member of a younger generation toward a member of an older generation. It is, of course, not always given. But exceptions are spoken of with disapproval. In rituals, respect is given with few exceptions. In many ceremonies this involves touching the feet of the elder. A man should not grow a moustache before his father's death, nor should he smoke or drink in his father's presence. Public disagreement with an elder relative is considered so disrespectful, as to be almost impossible.

The distinction between elder and younger relatives of the same generation (siblings or cousins) has many of the behavioral aspects of the generational distinction. It is not, however, obeyed so rigorously. For instance, public fights between brothers are frequently encountered.

Younger siblings must get express permission to marry from elder siblings of the same sex. It is also expected that the older brothers will take a responsible role--financially and otherwise--in marriage arrangements for their younger siblings. It is therefore considered bad form for an elder brother to leave a joint household before the younger siblings are all married.

Parallel cousins of several degrees of collaterality and siblings are referred to by the same terms, in accord with principles of Dravidian kinship terminology. Cross-cousins and affines of the same generation are referred to by another set of terms.[2] The most important distinction

---

[2] "Parallel" kin are related through siblings of the same sex: e.g., the children of two brothers. "Cross" kin are related through siblings of different sex: the children of a brother and sister. Both types of relationship can be extended out by degrees.

between the two categories is that the former are not marriageable, whereas the latter are. Thus, the two categories have also been called "kin" and "affines," or in-laws. (Dumont 1953). Cross-cousin marriage is considered desirable.

The Kannada term for a patrilineal descent group is *daayaadi*. The lineage includes agnatically related males, their wives, and their children. (Unmarried daughters are included, but married daughters tend to merge with their husbands' *daayaadis*.) The *daayaadi* share the same house god; they are also equally subject to birth and death pollution within the lineage, as well as to curses on the line. They share common ancestors and generally worship them in common by attendance at each other's houses during the annual ancestral feast. Among Brahmins, it occurs on the day of the death of parents of living individuals; among non-Brahmins all lineal ancestors are equally worshipped at a single annual festival, *pitra paksha*, or *maalada habba*. (See Chapter 8 and Hanchett 2022, Ch.7.)

A distinguishing fact of the relationship between affines is the belief (not always just a belief) that if the husband's relatives are not treated with sufficient ceremony, the married daughter will be mistreated. This pattern starts at the wedding itself, which takes place at the home of the bride.

The ideal relation between the sexes is seen as one of complete dependence by a married woman on her husband. Preparatory to this, she is expected to maintain a dependent relationship on her father and her brothers. Signs of this subservience are (1) never speaking the husband's name, (2) never addressing him directly in public, and (3) always walking behind him.

In fact, women are in a position of permanent dependence on males, because, according to traditional law, they cannot own property. (They may, however, hold it in trust for their minor sons.) Modern law has declared the right of women to inherit property, but few women have challenged tradition in the law courts.

Thus, the grandchildren of two brothers and their sons will address each other as 'brother/sister'

Marriageable and married women are expected to wear certain marks associated with their "auspicious" status. These include, with some caste variation, (1) a red mark (*tilak*) on the forehead, (2) glass bangles, and (3) flowers in the hair. Ornaments designated for married women (*muttaayide*) are (4) toe rings, (5) a black bead necklace, and (6) the *taali* pendant. The privilege of wearing these decorations is denied to widows.

The "pollution" presumed to be associated with menstruation is considered to be extreme. Harper (1964) refers to it as the justification for the female's inferior status. (One Chinnapura informant told me that women are voiding themselves of all their poisons and all their power at menstruation, and if it were not for menstruation they would be more powerful than men.) The restrictions on menstruating women are severe and strictly observed, at least among the Brahmins and non-Brahmins we knew. They are not allowed access to the "inside" of the house, and they must avoid touching anyone. They cannot wear the red *tilak* mark on their foreheads, nor should they comb or oil their hair. According to some reports, women are not even supposed to change their saris at this time.

The household is a group of people living together, sharing a common kitchen, in a structure with front and rear entrances. Most households are made up of nuclear or extended families, having only parents and one generation of unmarried children plus an elderly grandparent. But joint families are not uncommon. These consist of parents, one or more married sons and grandchildren, as well as unmarried children. Joint households vary in stability.

Rites of Passage

All categories of relatives are directly involved in each person's rites of passage, or life-cycle ceremonies, which always ritually symbolize a person's move to a new social status. Through ceremonial exchanges on these occasions, relationships among the various categories of kinsmen develop. (*Cf.* Dumont 1957a) Some rites of passage require the services of ritual specialists, and some do not. Rites of passage are celebrated by all castes, each in their own customary way. The most common ones are the following:

- Birth
- Naming

- First threshold-crossing of a baby (around six months of age)
- First haircut, for a boy
- Male initiation (especially important for Brahmins)
- Female's first menstruation
- Marriage agreement between two families
- Wedding ceremonies (multiple, can go on for one to three days)
- Consummation of a marriage
- Bride moving to her husband's house
- Ceremony at the seventh month of pregnancy
- Funerals and other death ceremonies

The Hindu Home and Kitchen

The Hindu home itself is not by any means taken for granted as a natural formation. Its continued existence is seen as being dependent on supernatural support. It is necessary to reaffirm this support through constant effort. Much of the effort involved in this is women's work.

The Hindu home usually has a shrine containing the house gods. The shrine is invariably in the kitchen, next to it, or in a room or closet entered through the kitchen. The kitchen is considered to be the most interior part of the house.

In fact, a distinction is made in Kannada houses dividing them into three parts: the verandah, the "outside," and the "inside." The most exterior is the verandah (*jagali*), a raised step that extends across the entire width of most houses. The verandah is a place from which it is permissible to meet with people of much lower castes. When it is necessary, such people (even Harijans) are allowed to take food or to sleep on the verandahs of houses of higher caste families.

The front room of the interior of the house is accessible to most visitors. Even so, it is usually defined as being "outside" (*horagaaDe*), and it is not a serious matter if it is somehow polluted. Guests are usually served food in this section. However, it is also the section in which the women of the house must spend the days of their menstrual pollution.

The kitchen (*aaDige mane*, literally "cooking room") and adjoining rooms, then, are "inside" (*(v)oLagaaDe*). It is rare that a person who is not of the householder's caste is allowed "inside." One of the exceptions is that Brahmins may come in for certain ritual purposes. And sometimes out of friendship an exception will be made, as it was sometimes made for us. The exact degree to which outsiders are proscribed from coming "inside" varies from caste to caste, but if the prohibition is broken, elaborate purification rituals will be required, even when the intruder is of "higher" caste than the householder. The reasons Hindus give for this prohibition is the presence in the kitchen of the shrine of the house gods. It is thought that the gods will be offended at the presence of an outsider.

"Inside" is always a marked area. Even in the smallest houses, there will be a wall separating the "inside" of the house from the "outside." This is not necessarily a ceiling-high wall, but may be of chest height or lower.

In addition to being the shrine of the house gods, the kitchen is also of course the place where most cooking is done. And, in view of the elaborate restrictions on commensality with various categories of outsiders, it is not surprising that the kitchen is protected in this way.

Diagrams of three typical houses are attached below, with other illustrations.

Human-Supernatural Interaction

The Sanskritic gods most widely worshipped in Chinnapura are Vishnu (as Narasimhasvaami), Lakshmi, Siva, Ganesha, and some minor deities. As was mentioned above, there is a temple for Vishnu as Narasimhasvaami inside the Brahmin section of the village.

Lakshmi (the goddess of wealth), Ganesha (for auspicious beginnings), and Sarasvati (goddess of education) are the trio whose lithographed pictures adorn the walls of even the poorest houses.

Siva is worshipped in the shape of a coconut, often resting in a bowl which is seen as the representation of Lakshmi, his consort. The sexual symbolism of this combination is self-evident to the local worshippers as to the outsider. (But it is also pointed out that the coconut has three markings, or "eyes," as does the god Siva.) Ganesha is often worshipped as *benuvaNNa* in the form of a cone of cow dung.

Two supernatural beings of great importance in Kannada dramas of the Hindu epics are Naarada and Sanimaahaatma. Naarada is a friendly sower of discord. He is not worshipped, but human trouble-makers are often referred to by his name. Sani is an astrological force, one of the nine planets, the one known to us as Saturn. He is a trouble-maker, and in a story whose format is strikingly similar to the Book of Job, there is a prologue in heaven in which Sani plays the same role as Satan does in the Biblical romance. The story is read occasionally at Brahmin ceremonies. Hanuman, the monkey king, *anjaneyya* in Kannada, is seen as an intercessor, a powerful saint, rather than a full-fledged god.

There are two major local deities that are generally worshipped in this region: Byadaramma (also called Mastiamma) and Mari or Maramma. They are both females, and both take sacrifices and offerings of full meals from a wide range of castes. As I have mentioned above, an annual Maramma festival involving buffalo sacrifice is a common element in South Indian village life. (*Cf.* Whitehead, 1927). Byadaramma is not usually a village goddess. Rather, she is more often worshipped by specific lineages.

Even the most western-oriented of the villagers believes in beings that we would call ghosts. These are recognized as part of a scale of beings that start at the high gods and include lesser gods, ghosts, people, and animals. Human interaction with supernatural beings is of course highly ritualized and shares many features in common with interaction between different categories of human beings.

As Harper (1964) has pointed out, the tripartite division of the supernatural bears too much resemblance to the tripartite caste division to be a coincidence. The *deevaru* are Sanskritic deities. The *deevates* are local deities, probably of Dravidian origin. And the *devvas* are what we would call demons or ghosts.

The Sanskritic deities are usually serviced by Brahmin priests. However, there are also temples serviced by various non-Brahmin priestly groups. In addition, there are temples whose priests are members of non-Brahmin and Harijan castes with a lineage tradition of special dedication to the god. There are also shrines of certain lineages where family members do the servicing. Temples exist in every A.K. colony. In addition, images are kept and decorated in almost every home.

The Sanskritic deities are considered to be vegetarian, although the eating of meat is often associated with their temples.

The *deevates*, local deities, are usually consumers of meat. The significance of this is emphasized by Dumont (1959), who calls attention to the structural implications for the Brahmin/Shudra division.

The *devvas*, judging from the terror felt toward them, are surely believed to be consumers of human flesh.

Food plays as great a role in human-supernatural interaction as it does in human interaction. I will discuss associated ritual behavior in subsequent chapters, especially Chapter 6.

Three Organizing Concepts: Dignity/Honor/Respect, Evil Eye, and Purity/Pollution

Before discussing some details of the behavior associated with vessels and cooking, I shall briefly define three concepts which deeply influence treatment of foods and food or other exchange behavior in Chinnapura. These are "dignity/honor/respect,"" the "evil eye," "purity" and its converse, "pollution."

The concept of *mariyaadi*, meaning "dignity," "honor," and/or "respect," is an important aspect of much behavior in relation to food. Food and utensils--like representations of gods, or like books--must be properly honored. Certain of these practices clearly have hygienic aspects, but the format throughout is parallel to treatment of human beings of superior social position. For instance, if one's foot touches the body of a superior person, then it is necessary to touch that person with the right hand, and to touch one's own eyes in turn. This amounts to a very great apology. (It is not necessary for a superior person to apologize in this way to an inferior.) Similarly, if one touches a pot or serving dish with one's foot, it is necessary to make the same gesture toward it. While eating, one must always be in a seated position, in order to show proper "respect" for food. This is especially true in the case of true meals, or *uuTa*.

It is also important to be aware of the idea of *drishTi*, "the evil eye." Under no circumstances should food in one's possession be seen by those who are not going to partake of it. In fact, if one person admires some fruit that another is bringing home from the market, the possessor is under an obligation to present him with some of it. This is considered to be the only means of preventing the whole lot from being spoiled by the evil eye. Similarly, in auspicious ceremonies it is necessary to avert the envious (and therefore dangerous) glance of those in attendance by presentations of food and sometimes of money. It should be stressed that the evil eye can be cast inadvertently and the only way of avoiding it is to give a gift to the observer. Under no circumstances should a person eat in the presence of those who are not also eating. Informants say that the person eating would surely get a stomach ache if he did so.

The terms *maDi* and *mayLige* refer to states of ritual purity and impurity, respectively. The person who prepares food should be appropriately pure. Menstruating women are of course prohibited from food preparation. Only a man is pure enough to prepare food destined for most deities. A purification ritual appropriate to each caste is performed by individuals preparing food.

Chapter 4

FOOD CATEGORIES AND CONCEPTS

In the spirit of Kenneth Pike's quest for "emic" understanding, this chapter will review the principal food categories as defined in Chinnapura by Kannada terms. Most food-related activity, both daily and ceremonial, is organized with these linguistically labelled concepts in mind. Naming foods and distinguishing various ways of processing them inform meaningful actions involving them.

Since the variety of foods ordinarily available is the basis for behavior associated with food, we shall first present a classification and general inventory of raw food types. After discussing some Kannada food terminology, we shall proceed to identify some basic techniques of food processing in this region and types of meals. Locally recognized distinctions among cooked foods will be discussed. Concepts of "heating" and "cooling" foods also are basic to popular thinking. And, finally, we will review the local system of flavor distinctions.

Regarding general categories of "food" and "eating," there is a difference between this system and the one based on English vocabulary. No general word for food seems to exist in Kannada, although any of the several words for cooked rice can be used with this general meaning. An exact translation of "raw food" is probably best rendered as *beesillada ahaara* (uncooked victuals). But this is a learned Sanskritic expression, more a literary term than a commonly used one. There are several words meaning "to eat." They are the following:

tinnu - eat (imperative); to eat
uuTa maaDu - eat the food [a meal with rice] (imperative)
nungu - swallow (imperative)
kabaLisu - gobble (imperative)

mukku - eat (imperative) used only as an abuse[3]

The three major locally defined categories of foods are (1) Vegetables and Grains, (2) Dairy Products, and (3) Meats. Figures 1, 2, and 3, below, classify the contents of these categories in general terms and identify specific foods included in each category.

In the three figures several items distinguish *uurina* from *kaaDina* varieties, that is, "domesticated" or "wild" varieties. Linguistic relationships are clear: the term *uuru* is the general term for town or village, while the term *kaaDu* refers to the natural forest.

The division between "vegetarian food" and "non-vegetarian food" is most deep-cutting and striking. But the division between these two domains is not necessarily where any member of Western society would draw it. Eggs, fish, mushrooms, and meat are considered to be non-vegetarian items. And everything else, including such animal products as milk and honey, falls on the vegetarian side of the dichotomy. Some items are difficult to classify. They are *bella* (cast brown sugar), *henda* (palm toddy, a mild fermented beverage), *serapu* (distilled liquor), *huuNise* (tamarind pulp), tea and coffee.

The animal products repertory (identified in Figure 3) is more restricted than the other two, and more weight is placed on each item. In general, Figures 1, 2, and 3 represents a sequence that gradually moves from items locally defined as "pure" to "polluting" things, milk products being purest and beef being most polluting.

Certain categories of ingested items are <u>not</u> discussed here as foods. For example, items referred to as *avsti* (medicine or poison) are excluded from consideration. They are neither vegetarian nor non-vegetarian. The category *avsti* includes a number of items, *e.g.*, chameleons or monkey hands, that are considered to be useful when ingested for curative purposes. But the effects of ingesting such items have nothing to do with either nutrition or pleasure.

---

[3] *Editor's note:* Thanks to Professor Narayan Hegde for confirming this information.

Some ordinary foods, however, are seen as having either medicinal and poisonous effects. And medicines and poisons share with food the indigenous distinction between "hot" and "cold" qualities, because of the pervasive influence of ancient humoral theories of cosmic and physiological organization.

The set of basic food categories presented below is mainly a kitchen classification. It is not identical with categories associated with marketing. The categories presented below were originally elicited from an informant of the Fisherman caste. These terms have been drawn from answers to a range of questions such as, "*santeyinda (y)een(y)een togoNDbandri?*" (What did you bring from the market?) Or, "*ii aDige maaDok,(y)een(y)een beeku?*" (What do you need to cook this food ?) Repetition of the elicitation with members of other castes increased the range of items considerably, but did not involve any major departures from the basic structure as outlined by the original Fisherman informant.

Categories of Raw Foods

One major vegetarian food category is *dinsi*, dried seeds. It includes staples, oil seeds, and spice seeds. Staples of the local diet are covered by the general term *daanyadavsa, daanya* being "cereals" and *davsa* being "pulses."

The most important grains or cereals are rice (*akki* in Kannada) and finger millet (*raagi*). Rice (*Oryza sativa*) occurs in both dry and wet varieties. The wet rice is grown in flooded fields, and the dry rice, in non-flooded lands. Wet-land rice is called *batta*, and dry-land rice is called *hola batta*. The Indian English term "paddy" refers, as *batta* does, to unhusked rice. One crop of rice is grown each year in this area. Seeds are planted in June; seedlings are replanted in June and July; and the crop is harvested in December and January.

Rice is both a subsistence crop and, recently, a cash crop, because of shortages in other parts of Mysore State [Karnataka] [Karnataka]. Rice is the higher prestige crop, as we shall discuss later in connection with symbolic manipulation of foods. Rice also is processed in many more different ways than finger millet.

Finger millet (*raagi*), however, is more important than rice as a staple in this region, though it lacks the all-India prestige of rice. One crop per year of finger millet (*Elusine coracana*) is cultivated in dry land.

Other grains are less important, both nutritionally and symbolically. They include wheat (not grown in the area), which has a high prestige value and is used in certain ritual and festival foods. It comes from northern India and, more recently, from the United States. It is sold in markets or obtained from government relief shipments.

The term *jooLa* is applied indifferently to sorghum and maize. In this district it is ordinarily grown only as a livestock feed. However, it is a staple food crop in northern Mysore. Because of recent droughts, and because of cheap supply by way of the government, it has started to be used in poorer Chinnapura homes as a staple food.

Pulses make up the second most important type of agricultural produce. They can be used in three forms: (1) fresh (*hasi*), as a type of vegetable; (2) whole and dried (*kaaLu*); or (3) split and dried (*beeLe*). The term *daanya* (in Figure 1) applies only to the latter two. The three-way contrast, made in English, which distinguishes pulses on the basis of shape (*i.e.*, peas, beans, and lentils), is unknown in Kannada.

The most important pulses in the Chinnapura diet are *toogari*, or toor dal (*Cajanus cajan*), red gram (*Cajanus cajan*), and *huraLi*, horse gram (*Dolichos biflorus*). In meals, these are the most common accompaniments of rice and finger millet, respectively. In dry land, grams are grown between rows of millet. Grams also are grown in dry paddy fields after rice has been harvested.

Other important grams are *avare*, field beans (*Dolichos lablab*); and *uddu*, black gram (*Phaseolus mungo*), which is used sparingly in daily meals but is a major component of side dishes and snacks. *kaDLe*, Bengal gram (*Cicer arietinum*), and *hesarbeeLe,* green gram (*Phaseolus aureus*), also are widely used, occasionally substituting for red gram or toor dal in the daily meal.

The other category of vegetable products in Figure 1 is *hasipadaarta*. This term refers to fresh items, and includes what Westerners would call vegetables, fruits, and leafy greens. Roots or tubers are called *geNDe* in local parlance, but *gaDDe* in more standardized speech, as in the term *aalugaDDe/aalugeNDe*, potato.

FIGURE 1
Basic Categories of Grains and Vegetables

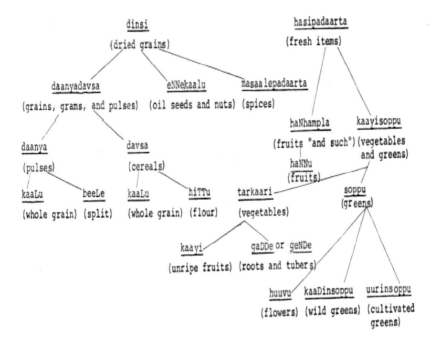

In Kannada ethnobotany four stages of fruition are distinguished. These are (1) *maggu*, bud; (2) *huuvu*, flower; (3) *kaayi*, unripe or green fruit; and (4) *haNNu*, ripe fruit or seed pod. (The seed is called *biija*.) Thus the category *kaayi* includes all fruits -- in the botanical sense of the term -- in their unripe stage. Coconut is *kaayi* (vegetable), rather than *haNNu* (ripe fruit), when the meat is moist. But dried coconut, in its fully ripened form, is called *koobri* and is regarded as a fruit. The category *kaayi* also includes such items as green peanuts (*nelagaDLe kaayi*), green bananas, and grams in the stage preceding full maturity. Cucumbers, *savtekaayi*, when fully ripe and yellow in color are called *savtehaNNu*.

Some members of the *kaayisoppu* category are cultivated as crops, while others grow wild and are gathered. In this region there are numerous varieties of edible plants, *kaaDinsoppu*, which grow wild in the fields and forests. They are regularly harvested by villagers to be used in cooking.

FIGURE 2
Animal Products: Dairy

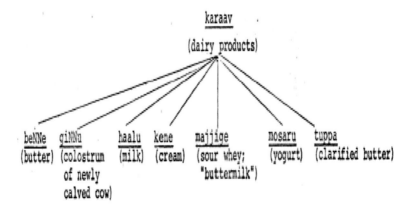

Dairy Products

Cow milk and buffalo milk are distinguished ritually, but under ordinary circumstances are both referred to by the same word, *haalu*.

They are different in taste, and buffalo milk has a higher butterfat content than cow milk. Some Brahmins and other castes own milk cows, but by far the greatest number are in the hands of members of the Peasant caste, who sell and process milk.

Milk is soured by adding a culture to boiled milk, for the production of *mosaru*, a yogurt type of product usually referred to in Indian English as "curds." Sometimes *mosaru* is sold, but it is usually churned for the simultaneous production of butter (*beNNe*) and sour whey or "buttermilk" (*majjige*), both products of great importance in the local diet. Butter is seldom used in the form it achieves in the churn. However, it is sold in that form on the assumption that it will be difficult to adulterate. Once brought into a home, it is boiled and skimmed into ghee (*tuppa* in Kannada), a product that is pure butterfat.

The milk of goats and sheep is not used by people in Chinnapura. The reason that villagers give are that (1) it is not correct to eat animals whose milk is drunk, or to drink the milk of animals whose destiny is slaughter; and (2) milk-fed lambs and kids grow to maturity faster than those deprived of their mothers' milk.

The colostrum of the parturient cow (called *giNNu*) is not fed to the calf; rather, it is used for the preparation of sweets.

Meats

Domesticated meats used by the people of Chinnapura are goat meat, sheep meat, chicken, pork, water buffalo, and beef. Only mature animals are eaten. Chickens are kept by many houses. They wander freely through the village eating garbage and excrement. They are apparently not fed by their owners. Their eggs are valued and treated as a kind of meat. Our European custom of mixing eggs invisibly in breads, cakes, and so on, is unknown at the village level.

Many of the villagers own goats that wander about the village and are taken out to pasture. No one in Chinnapura owns sheep. Possibly they require more attention than goats, since they are raised only in villages where people of the Shepherd caste live. Goats are usually raised for slaughter and sale, or occasionally for division among several families.

The same is true of pigs. These are usually bought as piglets at the Hassan weekly market and raised to maturity before being sold again for slaughter. Most of the pigs of the area are of the Asian variety, but at least one villager bought a European type of pig and raised it while we were residing in the village. (He was fond of comparing the soft pink creature to the visiting Americans, contrasting it with the hardy, dark-colored local creatures, both swine and human.)

The major purpose of keeping cattle -- according to village informants -- is the production of oxen, on which the rural transportation system depends. Accordingly, breeding is controlled with powerful oxen in mind. Milk breeds are unknown in this area. Cows are kept for milking, but their milk production is low by Western standards, in the range of one quart per day. Oxen are given special foods, whereas the villagers show much less interest in feeding cows. During peak work seasons cows are pressed into agricultural labor.

In theory only cows that have died a natural death are ever used as food. The fact is, however, that beef-eating Hindu castes and Muslims often buy cattle at the Hassan market for slaughter. There is also a lively tradition of cow theft for slaughter and sale. The people who sell their over-aged bullocks and dry cows at the market undoubtedly know their ultimate destination, but they claim ignorance.

Water buffalo cows ((y)emme) are the major local source of milk. Their yield is low by Western standards, a prize milker giving only a gallon a day. Male calves are sold off to Coorg, where, according to informants, heavy rainfall and deep mud make them the preferred draft animal. (I also observed their use in Kerala while touring there.) As with cattle, only carrion is acknowledged to be ordinarily eaten. The slaughter of buffaloes, however, is not universally considered to be an offense of the same order as cow slaughter.

The current legal prohibition on animal sacrifice is disregarded to a large degree, but it has had a restraining effect. It has virtually eliminated the public sacrifice of male water buffaloes to the goddess Maramma, to whom large numbers of buffaloes were traditionally sacrificed and consumed publically by Harijans. (See further details in Chapter 9.)

Probably the single greatest source of animal protein among non-vegetarian castes is fish. Individuals, fishing parties, and professional itinerant fishermen all catch fish. Fish are caught by net, by hook, by fish traps, by damming off parts of the river, and by the use of dynamite. They are caught in the river, in a nearby irrigation channel, and in flooded paddy fields.

FIGURE 3
Animal Products: Categories of Meats

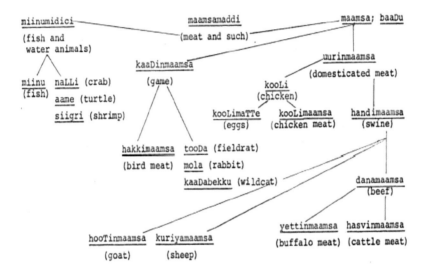

Hunting parties, individuals, and professional hunters catch small game. Since firearms are regulated, trapping by nets, and slaughter by bare hands, clubbing, slings, or bows is practiced. At the end of the harvest season groups go out to hunt field rats that live in the mounds that hold water in paddy fields. Other small game that are eaten in this area include wild and domestic cats, rabbits, and birds.

There are taboos on monkey meat (sacred to the god Rama), and squirrel meat. Local squirrels, like our chipmunks, are marked with a triple stripe thought to resemble the sacred markings of Vaishnavas (worshippers of the god Vishnu).

Mushrooms (*aNabe*) occupy a special place in this system of food categories. They are eaten only by castes that eat meat. However, they cannot be substituted for meat in ceremonial functions. Mushrooms are known to those who do not eat them as *naayikooDe* "dogs' umbrellas."

Variation in the Use of Some Kannada Food Terms

Like other Dravidian languages, Kannada makes use of standardized "echo words." An echo word is paired with a standard term, though the echo word itself may or may not have any meaning beyond, "etcetera." For example, "rice and so on," rice being *anna*, would be expressed, *anna ginna*; or "*cakli* and other snacks, etc.," *cakli gikli*. The phrase *haNhampla* (fruit, as in Figure 1), may be invoked when a man is asked what he ate on a fast day. Fruit is *haNNu*, but *hampla* has no meaning, as far as I could discover. In the term *daanyadavsu* (grains, grams, and pulses, as in Figure 1), on the other hand, both parts are meaningful.

One function of the presence of such echo particles is to make the boundaries of categories vague. The presence of "etcetera" in a term makes its reference essentially inarguable. In the case of *haNhampla*, for example, the presence of *hampla* makes it easy to provide space in the category for green mangoes (*maavin kaayi*) or another sour green fruit called *nelekaayi*, both of which might technically belong in the *kaayisoppu* (vegetables and greens) terminological category. Such ambiguity may represent a degree of conflict between the ethnobotanical and marketing or kitchen categories.

Some of the echo words have peculiar implications. For example, the phrase *maamsamaddi* (meat and such, as in Figure 3) is best translated as "meat and garbage." One hears the statement, "On that day we don't eat meat and stuff." The term *miinumidici* has the literal meaning of "fish and grasshoppers" and is used similarly. The pejorative implications of meat eating are made clear in such terms as these.

Certain words for food items seem to suffer from proliferation of terms, indicating positive or negative taboos concerning the items. Use of one or another of these terms may well be part of a social system of deference and respect. The items most often referred to in this way are meat, water, salt, and cooked rice. The term *maamsa* is the most common Kannada word for meat now used in Chinnapura. It is of Sanskritic origin, and evidently a recent borrowing into Kannada. Among Barber and Fisherman castes, however, the older word *baaDu* is commonly used, and it sometimes slips out in conversation. But it always was quickly corrected, at least in my presence.

In neighboring Kerala State, the word *baaDu* means "beef" in particular, rather than meat in general. There is evidently a tendency developing in Kannada to reserve *baaDu* also for beef, and the word *maamsa* seems to be replacing it as the general term as a result of this.

My Harijan informants never referred to meat as *baaDu* in my presence. Since this was an especially sensitive subject, I had to accept their statement that only the old people ever use the word *baaDu* for meat.

Among the Brahmins, water and salt are often referred to by their Sanskrit equivalents, or by more fanciful terms. At ceremonial meals the Iyengars sometimes use the term for sugar when offering foods including salt.

In addition to Sanskrit words, cooked rice is referred to as *uuTa* ("meal") or *kuuLu* ("food," archaic), or other words that have special meanings or are archaic in Kannada. A Harijan informant once used the word *cavre* instead of *anna* in referring to cooked rice. When questioned, he said that the word was Tamil (it is), and that he had used it as a joke. I accepted his explanation at the time, since the word is used in Tamil. At any rate, the tendency to use periphrasis when referring to cooked rice is evidently widespread. The word *anna* ("cooked rice") itself is apparently a borrowing from Sanskrit.

In certain cases the local food term differs completely from the standard colloquial Kannada term. The two most striking examples of this are the words for coriander, *saambaara* rather than *kootambari*, and for eggplant, *muLagaayi* rather than *baDnekaayi*. These local terms are used by all village castes and classes in conversational speech.

Food Preparation in the Home

In preparing food members of all castes respect some rules of proper behavior. Though economic differences and variation in customs produce many differences in cooking behavior from one house to another, and from one caste to another, there are some ideas which are generally shared on the subject of vessels and cooking.

The ideal cooking pot is made of gold, since the sensitivity of that metal to ritual pollution is considered to be the least among material substances. Its actual use, of course, is unknown except to maharajahs and in the great temples. Its susceptibility to theft makes it impractical even to those who value the purity of their food so greatly that they would be willing to squander their wealth on it. Second to gold is silver. Despite its high cost, many wealthy families do use it for eating utensils. Next in order is stainless steel. Although only recently introduced, it is very widely used in cooking and eating utensils. Copper and brass follow and are in fact the most common cooking utensils in any except the poorest homes. Iron cooking ware is required for certain cooking operations. Aluminum follows and is widely used. Most common of all are black, undecorated clay pots manufactured in a nearby village where people of the Potter caste live. They are sold in weekly markets or from door-to-door by Potters. Such pots are cheap, fragile, and extremely subject to pollution. Glass and porcelain also fall into this category.

Brahmin informants have told me that even the poorest among their caste will cook only in metal pots. One Smartha Brahmin informant told me that some cooking outdoors, for death or other inauspicious events, is done in clay pots among Brahmins. On ordinary occasions, however, "Even a beggar will use aluminum."

Once vessels have been used for cooking, they are in a state of *musare*, or contamination, a type of mild pollution. Stoves also become *musare* after cooking. Among Brahmins, this term is applied only to vessels or stoves that have been used for boiling rice. Thus, according to informants, if one touches a pot in which rice has been boiled, and then touches another vessel without washing one's hands, the second vessel and its contents also become *musare* or, in the case of stoves, one informant claims that she cleans her stove with water and cow dung after boiling rice, before cooking any other preparations on that stove. (Another informant told me, however, that it is not necessary to clean a stove that is *musare*, because rice fire is a god. Both were Smarta Brahmins, but the former was an "excessively" meticulous widow.)

Among non-Brahmins and Harijans the term *musare* is applied to all vessels that have been used for cooking, and is not restricted to vessels used for cooking rice, as it seems to be among the Brahmins.

The condition of *musare* contamination is not as serious as *mayLige* pollution. One informant explained that *musare* can be removed by washing one's hands even in the kitchen itself, whereas the *mayLige* pollution created by saliva contact (*injaLu*) while eating could not be washed away in the kitchen. One had to go out of the kitchen to wash hands after eating, since the ritual state of impurity created by the act of eating is much more extreme than that created by contact with food while cooking.

One Smartha Brahmin informant used the term *musare* in a slightly different sense than other informants did. During the festival called Shivaraatri it is necessary to "fast," by abstaining from cooked rice preparations. Smarthas prepare two main dishes to be eaten during this fast, one from wheat and one from pounded, soaked raw rice. But, according to this informant, if they ate boiled rice during this fast, they would become *musare*.

Among some castes who do eat meat there are often restrictions associated with its preparation. The most well-known case of this type in this region is the basis of the distinction between the *muula* and *daas* subcastes of the Peasant caste. Though both groups eat a wide variety of meats, members of the *muula* group typically have an extra stove in the "outside" portion of the house which is used for cooking meat.

Others of various castes occasionally explained special restrictions on meat cooking and eating. The Weavers of nearby Bandipur village seem to abstain from eating meat on Mondays, for example, since this is the day on which all animals (particularly bullocks) are given rest from agricultural labor, a day special to the bull that is the vehicle of the god Shiva. Further statements were made by others: that members of the Fisherman caste cook meat and fish only outside the house; that one Washerman caste family cooks all meat except pork inside, in the kitchen; that one family of the untouchable *maaDiga* or A.D. Harijan caste cooks meat outside of the kitchen, because their god is Chinchungatte Timma, the god of Tirupati.

I have also been told that it is not permitted to cook different types of meat together, *i.e.*, the meat from different animals. The distinction between milk animals and meat animals was mentioned above--that no animal is used both for its milk and for its meat. This latter practice seems

47

to be related to the fact that only mature animals are slaughtered, as I suggested above. The reason usually given is a folk-ecological one that all the milk of sheep and goats must be directed toward their own young in order to assure their fast growth. This contrasts with western practice, which includes the use of milk and the slaughter of young animals. The ideological element seems to be the deciding factor here: an animal from which one has taken milk becomes a kind of mother.

Seen as an event, an Indian family meal is arranged in time as an American family meal is arranged in space. In our case, everyone eats at the same time, and the head of the family sits at the head of the table. In the Indian case, the individual members often eat at different times, but it is expected that the head of the household will eat first.

Types of Meals

The most common morning greeting is, *uuTa aayta*? or more rustically, *uNDRa*? -- "Have you eaten?" If the individuals are friendly, they will pass the time of day asking each other the particulars of meals. The answers may or may not be truthful, depending on the conception the participants may desire to give of their lives. That is, a man who has just eaten meat will describe at length to a Brahmin an imaginary vegetarian meal or a status conscious individual will describe the wedding dinner he ate six months ago, rather than the gruel he actually ate today.

But, except for resident anthropologists, most people already have an idea -- accurate or inaccurate -- of what the other party must be eating and will pay little heed to the details of these reports. Such conversations correspond in general to our small talk concerning the weather. (Conversations about the latter are usually serious ones in Chinnapura, since bad luck can follow too cheery a comment.) Occasionally, an individual will ask the preparation of some dish that he hasn't heard of, and a lengthy recipe will be dictated.

There are two words which comprise the Kannada equivalent of the English word "meal." These are *uuTa* and *tiNDi*. These are roughly translated in this book as, "meal" and "snack," respectively, although in fact a *tiNDi* serving can include a large amount of food. The term *uuTa* refers only to meals containing specific cereal preparations: specifically, boiled rice (*anna*); red millet balls (*raagi mudde* in the higher dialect, *hiTTu* in the lower), and, among the poor, *ambaLi*, or *raagi* porridge, and *bambaLa*, water containing a small quantity of rice boiled with it. "Even *ganji*, rice water, can be *uuTa*, if there is nothing else," said one informant. A proper *uuTa*, then, should contain minimally one of the rice or red millet preparations mentioned above. This will generally be served with a spiced pulse preparation, usually that called *saaru*. Or it may consist of a cereal preparation served with a spice powder (*catnipuDi*), a spicy paste (*catni*), or spiced water. (See Figure 4)

The term *tiNDi* refers to an occasion on which any other type of food is taken, including bread, chappatis, or *raagi rooTi,* no matter in what quantity. The word *tiNDi* is a nominalization of *tiNNu*, "to eat," a word that applies to any kind of eating. Although it can be glossed in English as "snack," it may nevertheless sometimes be applicable to meals that would otherwise seem to be lavish.

On the other hand, *rooTi* (bread made from wheat or red millet) or *kaDabu* and *doose* (steamed dumplings and pancakes, respectively, both made with rice flour) are not *uuTa*. Nor are puffed, popped, or pounded rice (*puri, araLu,* and *avalakki*).

An elaborate set of food-sharing and food-exchange rules is in force, but these rules may be casually broken when people are partaking of *tiNDi*. Breaking the rules when partaking of *uuTa* is exceptional.

Although their defining characteristics are quite different, there are certain resemblances between the Kannada set, *tiNDi/uuTa* and the Hindi set, *pakka/kacca*. *Pakka* refers to food fried in clarified butter, and *kacca*, to boiled food. The term *tiNDi*, strictly defined, is in no way limited to fried foods. Yet, as it is possible to take *pakka* foods with individuals from whom one could not accept *kacca* foods, it is possible to take *tiNDi* from or with individuals from whom *uuTa* would be unacceptable. In the Hindi case, process is the defining characteristic, however, and in the Kannada case, format. This makes more detailed comparison difficult.

Fasting and Feasting

One typology within the domain of foods refers to the amount of food permitted. This can be regarded as a scale passing from extreme fasting, through ordinary eating, to feasting. The number of occasions when total fast (abstinence from all food and drink) is required are very small. Individuals who impersonate the ancestors at Brahmin death-anniversary ceremonies (described in Chapter 9) are required to have abstained from food since the previous evening's meal. Other cases of similar ritual implications exist. Some individuals, people with reasons to express extreme piety, report that they perform a total fast on occasions when partial fasting is required for others, as for instance, widows who take only water on *(y)eekaadasi*, the eleventh day of the lunar month.

The word *upavaasa*, "fast," usually refers to abstinence from *uuTa*, meaning millet balls (*hiTTu*) or boiled rice (*anna*). Although sometimes individuals restrict themselves to eating only fruit or milk on such occasions, most will eat pounded, puffed, or popped rice freely. On certain "fasts" rather complicated foods are specially prepared. One such fast is the *(y)eekaadasi habba*, an annual holiday. Brahmins usually fast on this day, which is to say, they prepare a dish called *kaDabu* (or *iDLi*, to the Tamil-speaking Iyengars), a rice and black gram dumpling, highly prized as a delicacy. Others fast on Saturdays, Mondays, and Thursdays, days sacred to individual gods.

Another type of fast, observed by non-vegetarian castes, does not call for abstinence from *uuTa*, but only from meat. These include some days of wedding rituals and certain festivals. These days are usually followed by a day on which a meat feast is required. Others abstain from meat on the weekly god days, for Siva on Monday, *e.g.,* and sometimes for other house gods.

Individuals sometimes take a vow to a specific deity, that they will avoid meat if a certain request is granted. In a few cases, such a vow may result in permanent abstinence from meat eating. Nevertheless, a person's caste-mates may regard this practice as a fast, since it is expected that his/her normal food includes meat.

Fasting, in the sense of avoiding certain types of foods, is one method of achieving a state of ritual purity (*maDi*) that is greater than the normal state. For example, in Bandipur village, the Harijans achieve a state of *maDi* by fasting before the annual temple cart procession, during which they mingle relatively freely with members of other castes. They are generally regarded by others as something better than "untouchable" on this day because of the fast which they perform. Just as cooking rice can make a pot *musare*, or "polluted," so also eating boiled rice puts an individual into a somewhat less pure condition than eating other foods.

The word for ordinary quantities of food is *nickaTLe*; and a banquet is *heckaTLe*. It is always possible to know when a feast has taken place in houses that can afford to have plantain leaves brought: they are visible in the gutters outside the house the next day.

A banquet is marked by formal arrangements: among Smartha Brahmins, for example, sugar on the leaf and *tovve* (cooked lentils without any sauce) on rice; among Iyengars, sweets at mid-meal; and in other groups, the presence of *paaysa*, a sweet, rich, pasty fluid. The location of each food and order of serving are specified by custom on feast occasions.

Distinctions Among Cooked Foods

The cooking repertoire is divided into two basic types of prepared foods: vegetarian and non-vegetarian. Only the vegetarian category is named in Kannada. The word that appears on restaurant signs to indicate vegetarian cuisine is *paalaahaara*, a learned word of Sanskrit origin. The ordinary reference to vegetarian food is *siipadaarta*, "sweet things," as in the sentence, *ii habbeadalli sipadaarte tintiivi* ("In this festival we eat only vegetarian food"). An even less affected usage is *siibaayi*, literally "sweet mouth."

In this section I shall discuss standardized items that appear commonly in ordinary and festival meals. Some other foods, particularly fried snacks and festival sweets (such as *hapLa* or "papadum," *sandige*, and others), will not be included here. These are numerous, varied, and associated with certain festivals, rites of passage, and entertaining or visiting affines (in-laws).

Since a class or prestige difference is involved in the vegetarian/non-vegetarian dichotomy, there is some tendency for non-vegetarians to use the vocabulary associated with vegetarian diets. In village conversation, for example, there is a tendency for both groups to use the terms *saaru* and *palya* whether they are talking about these vegetarian dishes or about their non-vegetarian counterparts, *(y)essaru* and *taLDa*. In the case of *saaru* little information is lost in such changes, since there are few differences between *saaru* and *(y)essaru*. However, *taLDa* and *palya* are quite different preparations, as I shall demonstrate below.

The most common accompaniment to boiled rice or *raagi* balls is called *saaru*. It is usually a thin soupy preparation containing boiled pulse, mixed spice powder, soured with tamarind juice, and finished with *(v)ograNe*. Optionally, it can contain some vegetables. (The same word can be used for a quite different but equally soupy meat preparation.)

If the preparation is of a special kind, its nature can be prefixed: *soppin saaru* is made with greens; *niir saaru* is watery or thin; *hurLi saaru* is made with horse gram.

The term *huuLi* is also a standard type of preparation. It is classed with *saaru* as *beeLe*, meaning "split pulse," but indicating "standard fare." (The word is identical with the word "sour," but has a different meaning.) It is usually thickened with coconut scrapings or rice flour.

A unique characteristic of South Indian cooking is referred to in Kannada by the term *(v)ograNe*. At the last stage of making of many preparations, boiled or otherwise, a small quantity of oil is heated. Mustard seeds are added to it; and when they pop, other spices, and sometimes dried pulses are fried in it. When the frying is complete, the mixture is added to the preparation.

Vegetarian main dishes are *saaru, huuLi,* and *tovve* (as in Figure 4). The term *saaru* refers to a thin preparation, usually containing pulses boiled with a mixed spice powder, seasoned with *(v)ograNe*, and made sour with tamarind extract. The alternative, *huuLi*, is similar to *saaru* but is usually thickened with coconut scrapings or rice flour. Sometimes it is soured with buttermilk instead of tamarind; in this case it would be called *majjige huuLi*. The preparation called *tovve* is unspiced, cooked pulse removed from *saaru*. It is placed directly on rice on certain festival occasions.

The following are considered "side dishes" (*nanckoLLodu*). (1) *(v)ograNe* contains fired split pulses, often with fresh coconut scrapings. (2) *koosambri* is a preparation of chopped raw cucumber, soaked black or green split gram. (3) *paaysa* is a sweet paste, usually with a milk or coconut milk base, served at banquets. (4) *catni* is usually a raw preparation of coconut and coriander leaves with a strong *(v)ograNe*, but the term can refer to any highly concentrated spicy paste. (5) *gojju* is a vegetable preparation in which the vegetables are not boiled, but are fried in the *(v)ograNe*.

Preparations by non-vegetarians are referred to with somewhat different vocabulary. The non-vegetarian word equivalent to *saaru* is *(y)essaru*. It is essentially the same preparation as *saaru*. When used by villagers, *(y)essaru* is often a horse gram (*huraLi*) preparation, called *huLLikaaLessaru*. However, it can also refer to meat preparations, such as *kuriyessaru*, "mutton sauce." A thin preparation containing spices but no pulses is called *niiressaru*, "water sauce." One thickened with rice flour is *hondessaru*. A boiled vegetable preparation mixed with a *(v)ograNe* containing ground split pulses is known as *taaLDa*. The word *palya*, used by non-vegetarians, usually refers to a thickened meat preparation. A common preparation of blood, liver, lungs, and brains is known as *nelakari*.

A spicy paste, such as a preparation of tamarind pulp and chilies or other spices, is known as *kaara*, "spicy/pungent." It is distinguished from *catni* by the absence of coconut. It is sometimes the only accompaniment to the cereal preparation in daily meals (*uuTa*). The *hindi* preparation is a spice paste that differs from *catni* also in lacking coconut. It will therefore last for six months in dry storage, since coconut will turn rancid in dry storage.

Lévi-Strauss (1966) has argued that preserved or aged foods constitute a distinctive category in most world cuisines. From South India, we can include pickles in this category. Preparation of a pickle in this region begins with boiling oil and putting spices into it before adding the cold (fruit or vegetable) elements. It is basically a *gojju* type of preparation. The most common variety of pickle in this region is called *uppinkaayi* (literally, "salted vegetable"). Preservation of this pickle is carefully done, and it is eaten frequently as an accompaniment to meals and snacks. Pickles (*uppinkaayi*) are made in clay pots, since they will not set in metal. They are carefully protected against any outsider's touch and considered especially sensitive to pollution.

FIGURE 4
Characteristics of Common Preparations

Vegetarian Main Dishes (served on rice)	Boiled split gram (beeLe)	Boiled whole gram (kaaLu)	Ground rice	Fried gram	Soaked split gram	Raw Coconut	Cooked Vegetables	Sweet
tovve	X							
saaru	X						(X)	
huuLi	X		(X)				X	
Side dishes (nanckoLLodu)								
palya				X		X		
koosambri						X		
paaysa	X							X
catni				(X)		X		
gojju				X			X	
usli		X				X		
Nonvegetarian Main Dishes								
yessaru	X							
hondessaru	X		X					
Side Dishes								
taaLDa					X		X	

Another favorite type of pickle is called *nellikaayi*, named for the green translucent fruit (*Phyllanthus emblicus*) from which it is made. Incidentally, this fruit (eaten in its green, *kaayi* stage) is sacred to the god Krishna, and must not be eaten before the *ugaaDi* festival. Shortly after that festival, there is a *nellikaayi* feast, which marks the beginning of the time when this fruit can be eaten.

The pickle is considered to be one of the more delicate foodstuffs of this cuisine, in terms of ritual vulnerability. Pickled items must not be touched by any outsider to the household. Two important reasons are given for this prohibition: (1) they are kept in easily "polluted" ceramic containers; and (2) they are in fact easily spoiled by contaminating agents, such as mold. This latter reason may provide a practical basis for the ritual sensitivity of pickles to "pollution." There is a prohibition against menstruating women preparing pickles or touching pickle jars, because the pickles are expected to be spoiled if they do.

Rice is prepared in several different ways, in addition to being boiled. The common rice preparations are listed below:

> *puri* - puffed rice, prepared by dry heat treatment of husked rice;
>
> *araLu/aLLu* - popped rice, prepared by dry heat treatment of unhusked rice;
>
> *avalakki* - pounded soaked rice;
>
> *kuusalakki* - parboiled rice (*i.e.*, boiled as paddy and then husked), little used in Chinnapura, but important in other South Indian areas.

These preparations, especially the first three, are much used by the poor who cannot afford rice. They are also used as snacks by those who can afford rice.

Finger millet (*raagi*) is most commonly served in the form of large balls made from cooked flour. These balls are called *muDDe* or *hiTTu* (literally "batter or flour," respectively).

The System of Flavor Distinctions

Flavors (*ruuci*) are generally agreed upon. People speak of six basic flavors:

> *siihi* - "sweet"
>
> *kaara* - "spicy/pungent," *i.e.*, hot in the sense of peppery
>
> *huuLi* - "sour"
>
> *kahi* - "bitter"
>
> *uppu* - "salty"
>
> *ogaru* - "astringent"

The meanings of the first five flavors seem to correspond rather closely to their English glosses. The sixth is the taste of grapefruit or plain areca nut. A seventh flavor should probably be added to this list: *sappe*, "flavorless." The example usually given is unsalted rice, and many tales concerning the relations between the sexes begin with the neglectful wife forgetting to salt her husband's rice and feeding him a flavorless meal. But the lack of any of the six basic flavors produces a result that is equally called *sappe*. For instance, European food, which lacks *kaara*, is *sappe*.

I was repeatedly told that a perfectly prepared dish contains ideal proportions of all the six flavors. When I asked informants to apply this theory, however, they usually spoke vaguely. They were especially vague regarding the place of *ogaru* in the diet.

"Hot" and "Cold" Foods

Most foods are seen by Hindus as either "heating" or "cooling." The principal Kannada terms for these qualities are *usNa* and *siita*, respectively. "Hot" and "cold" are applied to the description of foods, but they are also part of the ancient humoral medical and cosmic system, which describes the universe as being in a precarious state of balance that can be disturbed by excesses of either heat or cold.

Numerous interviews with Chinnapura informants indicate that excesses of either hot or cold foods are assumed to cause dysentery or respiratory diseases, respectively. These beliefs are incorporated into Hindu medical practice, and in case of illness, the first question that an ordinary Hindu asks, no matter what other treatment is given him, is, "What may and may I not eat?" Some foods are considered to be neither hot nor cold; thus I have indicated a category of "neutral."

Interviewing on this subject revealed a great number of differences in the details of beliefs among informants. That is, specific items would be classified differently by different informants, and they would debate and discuss the matter among themselves. But it is used by all as an organizing framework, and its existence as a scheme is in some ways more important than the entries themselves.

Degrees of heat and coolness are named. Extremes of either are considered to be harmful, according to my informants. The terms used in these discussions were: *curuku*, "burning;" *usNa*, "heating;" *tampu*, "cooling;" and *siita*, "excessively cold."

It is generally agreed that people with different *guuNa*, or "natures," will experience different effects from particular foods. Thus, I was advised, it would be impossible to state a fixed rule that would apply uniformly to all persons. Signs of too much "heat" in the body include eye burning, stomach ache, itches, and bloody discharges. The bad effects of "cold" include sore throat, colds without fever, and coughing. According to one Brahmin informant, the best flavor is associated with preparations which are neither too hot nor too cold, since these qualities affect health.

A list of some common foods, identified as heating or cooling by the indicated number of informants, is in Figure 5. The lack of uniformity on most foods was notable, although everyone had some way of classifying all foods as either "hot" or "cold."

Foods for Supernatural Beings

The offering of food is thought to draw supernatural beings into the inanimate stones and images that represent them. The image and the meal are sometimes covered together with a cloth for a short time, during which the deity is considered to have consumed the meal. The food offering is then regarded as god's "leftovers," and is distributed to the worshippers. Items of all sorts—most often foods and flowers--that are distributed in this way, after being offered to a god, are known as *prasaad*.

Meals offered to gods are known as *yeDe* among Brahmins and *taLLige* among other castes. Brahmins also use the term *nayveedya*, and for other castes the equivalent term is *cerapu*. These latter terms can apply to the ingredients from which the meals are prepared as well as to the meals themselves.

FIGURE 5
Ten Informants' Judgments: "Heating" or "Cooling" Properties of Common Foods

Food Items: Kannada	English	Number of Judgments As: Heating	Cooling	Neutral
Pulses				
avare	field bean (Dolichos lablab)	2	3	3
hesaru	green gram (Phaseolus aureus Roxb.)	0	9	0
hurLi	horse gram (Dolichos biflorus)	10	0	0
RaDLe	Bengal gram (Cicer arictinum)	2	1	5
togari	red gram (Cajanus cajan)	0	5	3
uddu	black gram (Phaseolus mungo)	2	4	2
Cereals				
akki	raw rice	5	1	0
gavde	wheat	7	1	0
jooLa	sorghum	7	1	0
raagi	red millet	0	7	0
Oil seeds				
yeLLu	sesame	1	0	0
Spices				
arasina	turmeric	7	0	1
cekke	cinnamon	6	1	0
gasgase	poppy seeds	1	5	1
jaaykaayi	nutmeg	1	2	1
jiirige	cumin	4	4	1
laviinga	cloves	6	1	0
meNasu	pepper	8	1	0
meNasinkaayi	chillies	5	1	2

FIGURE 5
(continued)

Food Items: Kannada	English	Heating	Number of Judgments As: Cooling	Neutral
Spices				
mentya	fenugreek	0	8	1
saambaara	coriander*	3	6	1
saasave	mustard seed	2	0	0
suNTi	ginger	7	1	0
uppu	salt	2	1	4
Fruits				
baaLehaNNu	banana	0	1	0
halasinhaNNu	jackfruit	1	6	0
huuNisehaNNu	tamarind	6	1	0
maavinhaNNu	mango fruit	4	3	1
parangihaNNu	papaya	5	1	1
TameeTohaNNu	tomato (ripe)	0	5	1
Flowers				
nuggehuuvu	nugge flower	3	4	0
Vegetables				
baDNeKaayi	eggplant	6	1	2
budgumbalakaayi	ash gourd	3	2	1
halasinKaayi	green jackfruit	3	3	1
kaDLekaayi	peanuts	0	4	3
koobri	dried coconut	0	3	3
koosu	cabbage	5	2	0
maavinkaayi	green mango	4	4	0
muulangi	radish	7	1	0

* All "hot"-identifying informants stated that if coriander is roasted, it becomes cold.

FIGURE 5
(continued)

Food Items: Kannada	English	Number of Judgments As:		
		Heating	Cooling	Neutral
Vegetables				
nellikaayi	tree berry	2	0	0
savrekaayi	squash	2	4	2
savtekaayi	cucumber	5	4	0
TameeTakaayi	tomato (green)	0	6	1
tenginkaayi	coconut	3	1	3
Roots				
aalugaDDe	potato	4	2	2
beLLuLLigeNDe	garlic	8	0	0
uLLigeNDe	onion	1	8	0
Greens				
daNTinsoppu	Amarantus gangeticus	1	7	0
mentesoppu	Trigonella foenumgraecum	0	7	0
sapsiigesoppu	Peucedanum graveolens	3	3	1
saambaarsoppu	Coriander leaves	4	2	1
Milk Products				
majjige	buttermilk	1	6	2
mosaru	curds	2	8	0
tuppa	clarified butter or ghee	4	4	0
beNNe	butter	0	6	0
	(buffalo butter)	2	0	1
	(cow butter)	1	3	0
haalu	milk	7	0	0
	(buffalo milk)	1	0	0
	(cow milk)	0	1	0
haalu	unboiled milk	1	5	1

FIGURE 5
(continued)

Food Items: Kannada	English	Number of Judgments As: Heating	Cooling	Neutral
Meats				
hasvinmaamsa	beef	1	0	0
kuurimaamsa	sheep mutton	0	1	0
hooTimmaamsa	goat	0	1	0
		1	0	0
Processed foods				
anna ganji	boiled rice water	0	1	0
avalakki	soaked, pounded rice	2	2	1
araLu	popped paddy	1	6	0
hurugaDLe	roasted Bengal gram	5	0	2
kusuvalakki	parboiled rice	0	7	0
puri	puffed rice	0	7	0
bella	brown sugar	6	0	0

Meals prepared for offering to supernatural beings are highly formalized. Certain preparations must be offered in strict arrangement, on plantain leaves if possible, or on dried-leaf plates, if the former are too expensive or otherwise not available.

The word *kuuLu*, an old word for food, is a term often used for a meal with inauspicious or death-related associations, as for instance, foods for ancestors. For example, it occurs in the word, *hindekuuLu*, which refers to rice balls that are offered by certain castes to the ancestors, and which are actually eaten by crows.

Food offered informally to minor deities, "the offering of a portion of the daily meal of ghee, boiled rice, etc., to creatures of all description" (Kittel 1894), is *bali*. It is usually eaten by dogs. It is not offered in the form of meals. During the village-level *jaatra* festival in nearby Bandipur village, one of the daily rituals is the dropping of a boiled rice and green gram mixture (*pongal*) at nine points in the village streets, where minor deities are thought to be temporarily staying. It was understood that the offering had been accepted when it was consumed by dogs. Chapter 9 presents further details on foods for supernatural beings.

Chapter 5

CASTE IDENTITIES, CASTE STEREOTYPES, AND CUSTOMARY FOODS

Food habits constitute a major part of the identity of every caste and sub-caste, both in the eyes of outsiders and for the groups themselves. Food customs and eating habits are used to define the Brahmin/non-Brahmin/Harijan distinction. They also are used to distinguish castes and sub-castes from each other. Some of these clearly are statements of "purity" or "impurity" *vis-à-vis* other groups, but others seem to communicate distinction, separation from other groups, or simply identity of the group, more than any ranking judgment.

Distinctions are made between and within castes and caste groups primarily on the following grounds: (1) Treatment of a particular food; (2) Patterns of fasting on certain days of the week, month, or year; (3) Eating different types of meat; (4) Cooking meats "inside" (in kitchen) or "outside" of the house; (5) Eating while sitting in separate lines at feasts (Eating "together" with another person means sitting side-by-side: thus the importance of sitting in lines at feasts.); (6) Order of eating at feasts - - higher castes first; (6) Patterns in the cuisine itself; and (7) Foods avoided.

I heard some version of the following statement about the food habits of animals and people several times in Chinnapura. It was usually made by informants of the Peasant caste, but also occasionally also by other non-Brahmins:

> The elephant lives on grass. He is slow to lose his temper, wise, forbearing, and long-lived. The tiger lives on meat. He is quick to lose his temper, clean in his habits, and protective of his own. The pig lives on filth (*holasu*). He is stupid, stubborn, and lazy.

The Brahmins live on vegetables and are like the elephant. The tiger is like the Peasant. And the Harijans are like the pig, for they live on filth.

Ideas about Food and Character

The Kannada term for "character" or "personality" is *guuNa*. The above statement describes common personal or character stereotypes which are generally used in this region to differentiate castes, together with their food practices.

A local Brahmin described the character differences resulting from habitual use of three major grains: finger millet, rice, and wheat.[4] According to him, finger millet is the food of the lower classes, and has a "cooling" effect on the character. Wheat, a food eaten only by the middle classes, is heating, and therefore makes possible higher mental and physical labor. Consumed together with ghee, it is neither heating nor cooling. Rice is slightly heating, and therefore suitable for study and mental labor, and it must be taken together with ghee and grams to modify this effect.

It should be noted, incidentally, that finger millet is the standard food in non-Brahmin households, even the wealthiest. Rice is reserved for guests and special meals, though in some houses rice and millet are both served for ordinary meals.

Drawing on a Sanskritic distinction, an Iyengar Brahmin informant once presented me with a similar three-part scheme relating food and character. He said, there are three types of diet:

> *(1) satvikaahaara*, which consists of vegetables, fruits, and milk products, avoids forbidden vegetables (such as onion and garlic), is lightly spiced, and produces a character completely in control of the passions;
>
> *(2) tamasaahaara*, which is a diet in which the precautions of *satvikaahaara* are not followed; spicy *(kaara)*, sour *(huuLi)*, and salty *(uppu)* foods are consumed; and food consumption

---

[4] It may be that opinions regarding wheat are left over from the time of Muslim rule in Mysore, since wheat is not generally cultivated in South India. It is of course extremely important in the other parts of India, such as the North and West.

is undisciplined. Persons who eat this type of food are easily angered, and otherwise susceptible to their emotions.[5]

(3 *rajasaahaara* is a diet of liquor and meat, which actually provokes the passions. Persons who eat this type of food are "slaves" of their senses.

Another Iyengar informant explained to me that there are three kinds of people, and their needs are different. "Brahmins are highly educated, and it costs them more to live than other people, since they need more luxuries," he said. "The Shudras (non-Brahmins) can live simply. They eat coarse foods, and their need for money is very little. The Harijans, on the other hand, are like people of a different religion. In fact, they are not really Hindus. They are like animals, and like animals, they do not really need anything special that civilized beings require. Furthermore, they live on carrion: nowhere else in the world is there a people who stoop so low as that," he shuddered.

There is a perceived association between physical strength and meat-eating. Of all the meats, beef or buffalo meat is considered to be the most "heating," producing the greatest physical strength. For example, a Washerman caste informant told me that the reason that the Harijans are physically so strong is that they eat the male buffalo meat at Maramma sacrifices. I was surprised to hear this type of statement about meat from the Brahmin priest at the local Narasimha temple. He told me that the god he serves is not so strong as Maramma because the god eats only curds, rice, and other vegetarian food, whereas the goddess gets regular animal sacrifices. He explained that because of this difference, Mararnma could protect the village more effectively than Narasimha could, and that her range of potency was probably as much as two miles, whereas Narasimha could probably reach no farther than the boundaries of the village.

While Harijans are considered by others to be strong and prone to violence because of their diet of beef and millet, non-Brahmins are objects of a different character stereotype. I once sat in on a discussion among a group of Peasants on the subject of Brahmin/non-Brahmin differences. It was generally agreed among them that the Brahmins were

---

[5] It should be noted that discipline in consumption of food is the model for discipline in other areas of life.

more intelligent than the people of other groups, and the country is falling apart because the non-Brahmins are not smart enough to rule.[6] One Peasant informant said during this conversation that when a Brahmin woman is pregnant, she will eat apples, grapes, almonds, the sweetest variety of banana, tomatoes, and tangerines. Therefore, her children will be sweet and smart. But the Peasant wife will eat mud (*gooDemaNNu*) and field mud (*gaddemaNNu*), and her children will have mud sitting inside their heads.[7]

Foods and Caste or Sub-caste Identity

Food customs, together with other practices form one basis of self-identification. A sub-caste statement from a Barber informant of the *muula* Barber group was, "The *daas* Barbers build a wheel in their wedding ceremony and drink toddy, so we don't take boiled milk from them, and we won't marry girls of their caste."

Another example is the simple distinction between the basic spice powder (*masaala puDi*) of the Smartha and Iyengar Brahmins. The main difference between the two powders is that the Smarthas fry the coriander seeds before grinding them, and the Iyengars do not. Most members of both groups see this as a significant difference between the food habits of the two Brahmin groups. (Presumably, this difference comes up during daily exchange of recipes.)

Another type of difference based on use of a particular common preparation is that identified by a Peasant informant: "We non-Brahmins only make *biisibeeLe baat* (rice boiled with pulses and vegetables) for feasts. Other castes eat it at other times."

---

[6] When I asked them how they could vote for non-Brahmins if they believed this, they replied that they do because Brahmins will favor only other Brahmins. During the time of Haidar Ali's and Tipu Sultan's (Muslim) rule in Mysore, the informant elaborated, there was one time when for half a day the reins of government fell into the hands of a Brahmin. In that half day, he created *jooDidaari* (land grants of whole villages to single families) and gave lands to all the Brahmin temples.

[7] Geophagy, the practice of eating mud and other non-foods during pregnancy, occurs in many parts of the world. Cf. Vermeer (1970).

For Brahmins as a group certain items are "forbidden" or *nisheeda*. As well as meat, this list includes tomato, cabbage, radish, snake gourd (*padvalkaayi*), onion, beet root, lotus roots (*tavar beetu*).[8]

I have mentioned in the preceding chapters that the *muula* and *daas* groups of Peasants have different practices regarding the cooking of meat--the former cooking it only outside the kitchen, and the latter cooking it inside the kitchen. The *muula* Peasants also claim that they do not eat pork, but I have seen males of this group eating it. Women of this sub-caste, however, do seem to avoid eating pork.

As I have mentioned above, Saiva groups (*i.e.*, those who worship primarily Siva or associated deities) tend to avoid meat on Mondays, as a type of meat "fast."

The Fisherman caste custom of eating fish on the day of ancestor propitiation and on the festival day for their patron goddess is also clearly a self-identifying food practice

At the level of the sub-caste distinctions in food practices, one major implication is in marriage arrangements. These pretensions of superiority (or at least exclusiveness) affect the bargaining process in marriage arrangements between sub-castes, but final decisions tend to be made on more practical bases.

Knowing Other Caste's Food Customs

One caste's socially-identifying patterns of food practice often are visible to members of other castes. The *muula* Peasants distinguish themselves from the *daas* Peasants, for example, by the fact that *muula* Peasant women will not cook meat in their kitchens. It is cooked only by men, and in an area defined as an "outside" part of the house. A display is made of this custom. And as a result, members of many different castes are quite aware of the *muula-daas* sub-caste division.

In collecting information about inter-caste food exchange patterns, I discovered that many castes were aware of a few (I thought) obscure sub-caste distinctions made among, for example, Toddy Tappers, or Shepherds. Statements would be made, such as, "The 'blanket' sub-caste of Shepherds eat pig meat," a *muula* Peasant informant told me,

---

[8] [*Editor's note:* Possibly also garlic]

explaining that he takes only a limited range of foodstuffs from this group. But he accepts all foods from the other Shepherd sub-caste. Or, "They eat pork and drink toddy," said one Barber informant, who also accepts all foods from the other sub-caste. Within the Toddy Tapper caste, one sub-caste (the *maddi iDiga*) is reputed to drink toddy and other liquors, and as a result is generally considered to be less acceptable than the other sub-caste, who do not have the reputation as being heavy drinkers.

One Muslim informant stated that no house should mix vessels for cooking meat with others, in explaining why he would not take a wide range of foods from *daas* Peasant houses (these are houses where pork is cooked in the kitchen). One Iyengar informant told me with great certainty that members of the Smith caste use garlic, onions, cloves, and other such items in their spice powder.

At all levels of differentiation (caste-group, caste, or sub-caste), groups have knowledge and opinions regarding each other's food customs. And there is evident a certain amount of competition to proliferate food distinctions as separators of social groups, even among people who are otherwise close to each other.

Substitutions: Mythical and Practical

A local legend demonstrates that different social groups must stick to their own traditional distinctions among foods they can offer and/or can accept. The story is that of a swaami from Sringeri who came to Chinnapura in 1965 or so and gave a *darshan* ("blessing from his presence") to 2000 people in the village square. For a contribution of 250 rupees he took food in the home of the elder of the two *jooDidaar* brothers. (My informant thought the swaami must make 750 rupees per day.)

This swami, according to this tale, once had given a *darshan* to the Nizam of Hyderabad (a Muslim), who had offered liquors and meats to a Hindu god. When the cloth cover was taken off of the food after the *puuja* "offering ritual," those meats had become fruits and vegetables, and the liquors had become curds, milk, and sherbet. That is, the Muslim offered his traditional foods, and the god partook of them through miraculous intervention--as <u>his</u> own traditional foods.

This legend raises the question of symbolic substitutions of food items, which also arises in relation to feeding supernatural beings. In some offerings, such as in ancestor propitiation ceremonies, a Harijan uses beef, while a Brahmin uses black gram or sesame. Most non-Brahmins use other kinds of meats, and Fishermen use fish. It may be that different aspects of the symbolism of animal sacrifice (or, at any rate, offering of meat) are represented by the different substitutes.

Since the vegetarian Brahmin system presents a wide range of non-interchangeable elements, we may guess that meat will represent several different (corresponding) things in non-Brahmin ritual. There may also be more than one position in the structure of Brahmin ritual offerings that corresponds to the use of meat in non-Brahmin rituals; or there may be other elements which can fill those positions in lieu of meat for non-Brahmins as well.

Chapter 6

FOOD EXCHANGE, PURITY, AND SOCIAL RELATIONSHIPS

Food sharing occurs within a larger social context. Patterns of giving and taking (or not taking) foods reveal common assumptions about social connection, social disconnection, and hierarchy. As Marcel Mauss's seminal work, *The Gift*, demonstrated conclusively, such exchange – he used the broadly meaningful French word, "prestations" – is the way that humanity frequently expresses and organizes relationships between clans, tribes, families, and other types of groups. This leads the observer to understand that the details of exchanges are quite important to participating parties. In the preceding chapter, we dealt with caste identities in particular, and the relation of food concepts or categories to the caste system as a whole. In this chapter I will discuss the principles of "purity" and "pollution" that strongly influence food exchange behaviors at certain points in the life cycle, and some roles of different types of food in exchanges.

Food Exchange and Ritual "Purity"

Several states of being or social conditions are generally assumed to affect all types of social interaction. These are usually summarized in discussions of "ritual purity" or "pollution." Such states are affected by cooking practices, general dietary habits, intake of foods while fasting or feasting, and of course by caste identity.

On the occasions of specific rites of passage and some other ritual events, for example, a family or household may be put into a condition of "impurity," during which its members should not give food to members of other families. These ritual states affect specified members of the kin group, and not others. And there are different terms (and rules) for the different types of impurity and separation.

When a baby is born into a house, members of the lineage of that baby are subject to a period of impurity called *puruDu* or *sutaka*. Lineage-mates (*daayaadi*) of the mother and baby-- *i.e.*, the father's agnates--are restricted from giving food to others for ten days.[9] (They can, however, eat together with other lineage-mates.)

Another period of impurity occurs when a daughter of the house begins her first menstruation. This event is considered to be similar in many ways to the birth of a baby, and the newly menstruating woman is called by the same term as a new mother: *baananti*. She is in this condition for eleven days, just as a new mother would be, and is given a special diet to protect her health, since she is considered to be in a delicate condition. At this time her *dayaadi* are also in a condition of *puruDu* impurity for eleven days.

When a member of a patrilineage dies, lineage-mates are in a condition called *sutaka* for ten days. As with birth impurity, those in the condition of *sutaka* are most definitely forbidden to give food to others. This state of impurity is removed by a ritual specialist, either a Brahmin or *aynoru* (member of a non-Brahmin priestly caste) at the end of the period. The end of this period is typically marked by a large feast held outdoors and attended by all who participated in the funeral. In Chinnapura and Bandipur most non-Brahmins and Harijans use the term *sutaka* for all of these states, rarely using the term *puruDu* at all.

Though these ritual conditions have the effect of separating "polluted" members of society from the rest, they are not as restricting as *mayLige* pollution. A menstruating woman, who is considered to be *muTTucettu* or *mayLige* (cf. Harper 1964), cannot give food to anyone. Anyone who touches her is vulnerable to become *mayLige* ("impure") as well and must bathe to remove this pollution.

---

[9] Babies are often born in the natal home of the mother, where she stays for approximately three or four months after the birth. However, the parents and siblings of the mother are not vulnerable to the full ten-day period of *puruDu* impurity, but only to a three-day period.

The conditions of *sutaka* or *puruDu* are not as physically dangerous to others as *mayLige*, and restriction on giving food is the primary method of separating them from others. The occasion of a death-anniversary ceremony puts a Brahmin household into a special food-exchange position. Though a ritual feast for *daayaadi* is a part of this ceremony, members of other castes have told me that they would never take food from a Brahmin house on the day of this observance. I heard this even from Harijan informants, who will generally take any category of food from anyone.

Non-Brahmin middle castes make offerings to their ancestors on one day each year, rather than observing death anniversaries (after the first year). On the day of this "festival, " called *pitra paksha* or *maalada habba*, Harijans are required to stay out of the non-Brahmin parts of the village altogether. But they are entitled to a share of feast foods on the day after the ancestor ceremony, from all houses that have performed it. I do not think that there is a general term for the impurity or separation of a house on such occasions as these.

There are many other occasions, of course, when food exchanges are required or at least extremely desirable. One Peasant house distributed *tiNDi* on the occasion of the birth of a calf. After the periods of birth and first menstrual pollution are over, a general gathering is desirable, and some foodstuffs (fruits, sugar, and betel, usually) will be distributed. Most "auspicious" occasions, *i.e.*, those not associated with death, are celebrated partly through distribution of snacks and other foods by the house involved.

Saliva Pollution (*injaLu*)

Left-overs, or *injaLu* (literally, "saliva"), are considered to be seriously polluting. This term is also used to refer to the impurity resulting from defilement with saliva, real or technically defined. Thus, for example, a plate from which one has eaten anything is said to be contaminated with saliva, and must be handled rather delicately, and certainly not brought into contact with others, lest it defile them.

In some ways a pot on the stove can be considered to be vulnerable to *injaLu* pollution, once food has been served out of it. Thus, a Brahmin woman (and probably women of other castes) should wait until her husband has been served before she serves herself, lest her

73

injaLu should somehow pollute the pot during the serving process. It is for this reason that a Hindu meal is typically served by one member of the household who does not eat together with the others: there would be considerable danger of *injaLu* defilement to the serving vessel if those touching it were also in the process of eating their meals. In spite of the fact that they are considered to be so totally polluting, *injaLu* foods of most types are generally accepted by Harijans from members of other castes.

Hierarchy of Food Types

In the food exchange system of Chinnapura different types of foods are appropriate to different exchange situations. These can be arranged on a graded scale, ranging from "raw" foods to left-overs. This scale indicates (in a general way) the degree of purity or pollutability of foods. In terms of susceptibility to "pollution," raw food is most secure. It is always possible for a person of high caste to accept raw food from others. Some persons seem to be more restrictive than others, as will be discussed below. But others can justify these exchanges easily, as one Brahmin informant did when I questioned him about accepting betel leaf from a Harijan: "After all, leaves are the goddess Lakshmi, aren't they?" In other words, all crops are God-given and God-blessed, at least in their natural forms.

The distinction between oil-cooked and water-cooked foods – or *pakka* and *kacca* -- so important in North India, is practically unknown in Chinnapura. Brahmins, however, are careful in their cooking arrangements to separate the *musare* foods--those involving boiling, and in particular boiled rice, as discussed above--from oil-cooked foods. In one house at least, a *musare* stove must be specially purified with cow dung before it can be used for cooking other foods. Yet for non-Brahmins, *musare* is simply the term for dirty vessels in which any type of food has been cooked.

A basic assumption in this food system is that accepting cooked food of any kind places a person equal to or lower than his host. It is customary to give cooked food to servants and to people of lower castes.

Meat and Other Non-Vegetarian Foods

As the practices of cooking it indicate, meat is often separated into a special category and considered somewhat ritually defiling. One of my most difficult problems in the field was to find out a cover term equivalent to the English word, non-vegetarian. This is not, of course, an ordinary word in English, but *naanvej* (non-vegetarian) is in fact an important element in the vocabulary of educated Indians. In fact, one of the most striking facts of Indian town markets is the presence of a well-marked non-vegetarian section, where meat, fish, and eggs are sold. It would logically be expected that in a place where the distinction is central, it would be expressed simply. At first I thought I had found the term when an informant told me, "On that day we don't eat meat (*holasu*)," *avattu holas tinodilla*. But further investigation proved that *holasu* meant "filth;" it was clearly not the item I wanted. The term presented in Chapter 4, *maamsamaddi*, was the nearest approximation that I could find.

Eating meat is discussed sometimes in veiled terms. If the term *holasu* ("filth") is not used, some other vague reference might be made. For instance, a man of the Smith caste spoke of his own Carpenter sub-caste as the *tinnovunnooru*, "the people who eat." As with "drinking" in English, the meaning of "eating" in this case had a specific implication, namely, the eating of meat. As I mentioned above in relation to kitchens and cooking, the Peasants distinguish two sub-castes according to where they cook meats: whether "inside" (in the kitchen) or in "outside" parts of the house.

Vegetarianism is generally considered to be a purer condition of existence than meat-eating. Most castes acknowledge this belief, in their practices as well as in their general assumptions regarding caste hierarchy.

The next chapter will summarize my information on inter-caste food exchanges and their hierarchical implications.

Chapter 7

FOOD EXCHANGE AND INTER-CASTE RELATIONSHIPS

It is common knowledge among students of the Indian caste system that commensality is restricted between members of different castes. Certain categories of foods (such as those discussed in Chapters 4 and 6) are appropriately given to members of other castes that are higher or lower than oneself, depending on the degree of perceived "purity" of those foods and those people. These phenomena have been discussed at length by Stevenson (1954), Marriott (1959), and others in the anthropological literature.

I gathered some data on inter-caste commensality rules in both Chinnapura and Bandipur. A total of 121 informants (59 females and 62 males), of 13 different castes, plus Muslims, were asked which foods they should or should not accept from members of particular other castes. Questions were phrased in terms of ideal behavior, not in terms of actual exchange practices. Responses were highly individualistic, both in terms of foods accepted and rejected, and in terms of relations to particular other castes.

The range of foods about which we asked is as follows: water (one's own cup), water (their cup), puffed rice or fried Bengal gram, betel leaf or nut, buttermilk, unpeeled fruit, peeled fruit, unboiled milk, coffee, a fried snack called *cakli*, a steamed dumpling called *iDLi*, *uuTa* meals, and lime for betel chewing.

Each informant was asked about the following castes: Washerman, Fisherman, Weaver, A.K. Harijan, A.D. Harijan, Oil-Presser, Brahmin, Barber, Shepherd (two sub- castes), Muslims, Lingayat sect members, Smith (vegetarian and non-vegetarian sub-castes), Peasant (two sub-castes, *muula* and *daas*), and Potter. These are the most common castes in the region of Chinnapura and Bandipur, although not all are represented in the villages themselves.

As I mentioned above, the responses to these interviews were highly individualistic, and there was considerable variation even among informants of the same caste. A brief example from my Fisherman caste respondents will demonstrate this point. Six people of this caste were interviewed, four females and two males. Two females and one male were chosen from each village. The Fisherman caste is generally considered to be low in the village social hierarchy: that is, very few castes will take a wide range of foods from them. And they are generally thought to be willing to accept foods from other castes.

Though no two Fisherman caste respondents gave exactly the same set of answers to our questions, each had a sort of pattern in his or her responses. That is, each informant had foods grouped into sets, and each set would be taken from a corresponding set of other castes.

For example, one woman stated that she would (a) take no foods at all from Harijans, Barbers, or Muslims; (b) only betel and unpeeled fruit (e.g., banana) from Washermen, Toddy Tappers, Weavers, or Oil-Pressers; (c) only betel, fruit, and puffed rice or fried gram from Smiths; and (d) all foods from her own caste-mates, Potters, Shepherds, Peasants, Lingayats, and Brahmins. Her responses are diagrammed in Figure 6.

The groups of castes thus separated can be said to form a hierarchical set, ranked in terms of degree of commensality. Each informant, however, had a slightly different set of caste-groups and different food groups to distinguish them. Interview results for all six Fisherman caste respondents are summarized in Figure 7.

FIGURE 6
Range of Foods Acceptable from Specific Castes
(Devamma, Fisherman Caste Female, Chinnapura)

May Accept	From Castes
No foodstuffs	Adikarnataka Harijan
	Barber
	Muslim
Betel and Unpeeled Fruit	Washerman
	Toddy-Tapper
	Weaver
	Oil-Presser
Betel, Fruit, Puffed Rice	Smith
All types of foods	Fisherman
	Potter
	Shepherd
	Peasant
	Lingayat
	Brahmin

FIGURE 7
Ranked Groups of Castes Distinguished by Foods Received
(Fisherman Informants)

Rank Order (Low--High)	Foods Acceptable	From Castes (Informants' groupings)
I	Fruit only (1 informant)	Harijan (3 informants)
	Fruit and Betel (2)	Harijan, Muslim (1)
	No foods (3)	Harijan, Muslim, Barber (1)
		Harijan, Weaver (1)
II	Fruit only (1)	Barber (1)
	Betel only (1)	Muslim (1)
	Betel and Buttermilk (1)	Barber and Muslim (2)
	Betel, Fruit, Puffed Rice (1)	Barber, Washerman, Toddy-Tapper, Oil-Presser (1)
	Betel, Fruit, Puffed Rice, and Peeled Fruit (1)	Washerman, Toddy-Tapper,
	Betel, Fruit, Peeled Fruit, and Unboiled Milk (1)	Weaver, Oil-Presser (1)
III	Fruit and Betel only (1)	Barber, Non-vegetarian Smith (1)
	Fruit, Betel, Puffed Rice (1)	Smith (2)
	Fruit, Betel, Puffed Rice, Lime (1)	Washerman (2)
	Fruit, Betel, Puffed Rice, Lime, and Peeled Fruit (1)	Shepherd (1)

(continued)

FIGURE 7
(continued)

Rank Order (Low--High)	Foods Acceptable	From Castes (Informants' groupings)
III	Fruit, Betel, Lime, Peeled Fruit, Unboiled Milk (1)	Shepherd
	Fruit, Lime, Puffed Rice, Unboiled Milk, Coffee (1)	
IV	All foods (2)	Fisherman, Potter, Peasant, Lingayat, and Brahmin (1)
		Fisherman, Potter, Peasant, Shepherd, Lingayat, Brahmin (1)
	Betel, Fruit, Puffed Rice (1)	Washerman (1)
	Betel, Fruit, Puffed Rice, Lime, and Peeled Fruit (1)	Smith (1)
	(Above) + Unboiled Milk (1)	Washerman and Weaver (1)
	(Above) + cakli (1)	Smith and Weaver (1)
V	Betel, Fruit, Puffed Rice, Lime, Peeled Fruit (1)	Potter and Weaver (1)
		Toddy-Tapper (1)
	Betel, Fruit, Puffed Rice, Unboiled Milk, Boiled Milk (1)	Shepherd (1)
	Betel, Fruit, Puffed Rice, Lime, Unboiled Milk, Peeled Fruit (2)	Shepherd--"Blanket" subcaste (1) only

(continued)

FIGURE 7
(continued)

Rank Order	Foods Acceptable	From Castes (Informants' groupings)
VI	Betel, Fruit, Lime, Puffed Rice, Peeled Fruit, Unboiled Milk (2)	Toddy-Tapper (1)
		Oil-Presser (1)
	Above + cakli, coffee (2)	Vegetarian Smith (1)
		"Blanket" Shepherd and Oil-Presser (1)
VII	All foods (3)	Fisherman, Oil-Presser, Toddy-Tapper, "Milk" Shepherd, Peasant, Lingayat, Brahmin (1)
		Fisherman, Oil-Presser, Toddy-Tapper, "Milk" Shepherd, Potter, Peasant, Lingayat, Brahmin (1)
		Fisherman, Potter, "Milk" Shepherd, Weaver, Peasant, Lingayat, Brahmin
	Betel, Fruit, Lime, Puffed Rice, Peeled Fruit, Unboiled and Boiled Milk	daas Peasant
VIII	All foods except buttermilk	Fisherman (own caste)
IX	All foods	Oil-Presser, muul Peasant, Lingayat, Brahmin

As can be seen from Figure 7, even in this relatively low status Fisherman caste, two respondents identified four differently ranked groups of castes; three identified seven; and one went so far as to identify nine degrees of commensality with different sets of castes. Furthermore, the castes which are placed in these ranked groups can only be said to overlap in a general way, and there are some extreme differences among respondents in placing particular castes. For example, one informant places the Weavers in the lowest group, whereas another indicated that he (a male) would take all types of food from members of the Weaver caste. Weavers are also found in groups II, IV, and V, in the "intermediate" range of the hierarchy.

It is, therefore, extremely difficult to identify a single hierarchy of castes on the basis of this information An attempt to do so might look something like Figure 8, below. Ranking distinctions are clear only at the "top" and the "bottom" of the scale, with Harijans and Muslims invariably low and Peasants, Lingayats, and Brahmins high. These latter three castes were considered to be legitimate sources of all types of foods by all six respondents, though some said they would take all foods from other castes as well.

FIGURE 8.
Caste Ranking -- Low to High – by Foods Accepted
(Six Fisherman Respondents)

Caste Name	Ranked In Group Number	All Foods Taken (# Informants)
Harijans	I only	None
Muslims	II, III	None
Barbers	I, II, III	None
Weavers	I, II, IV, V, VII	1
Washerman	II, III, IV	None
Toddy-Tappers	II, V, VI, VII	2
Oil-Pressers	II, VI, VII, IX	2
Smith	III, IV, VI	None
Shepherd	III, IV, V, VI, VII	4
Potter	IV, V, VII	4
Peasant	IV, VII, IX	6
Lingayat	IV, VII, IX	6
Brahmin	IV, VII, IX	6
Fisherman (own caste)	IV, VII, VIII	5

With some minor adjustments (such as placing the Fisherman caste together with Barbers and Washerman; and the Weavers generally with the Toddy Tappers and Oil Pressers), this hierarchical scale is similar to that abstracted from other castes' reports. Though this is a "low" caste, members of the Fisherman community seem to make the same distinctions among regional castes that other groups do. These distinctions are understood in terms of food exchange distinctions by each individual, but the exact understanding of details varies considerably.

Before discussing other types of food exchange among village social categories, I would like to mention a few points suggested by these data. In the first place, the data were elicited only as rules of behavior, and not as descriptions of actual behavior at all. The question addressed to the informant was, "Should you take this food from this caste?" and not "Do you take this food?"

I was hoping by this means to elicit an abstract view of a single ranking system, which might be shared by all members of this community, at least as an ideal. The responses from the Fisherman caste informants demonstrate that it was not possible to produce this desired result by this method.[10]

In regard to the foods themselves, another desired result was to establish that particular foods were always acceptable, and that others never acceptable. The set of thirteen basic food items was in fact adequately differentiated to enable each individual informant to create a personal ranking system based on food exchange. However, as Figures 6, 7, and 8, demonstrate, specific foods can be grouped in only the most general way. As with castes, the "bottom" (betel and unpeeled fruit) and the "top" (all foods) of the hierarchy are the only parts of it that are very clear. But these extremes are easily understood by ordinary observation of village life, and a more detailed, extensive survey was not necessary to achieve this result.

For these reasons, I feel that it is not necessary to present the remainder of these data here. Though they are extensive, they do not seem to be particularly enlightening beyond the points that have already been mentioned.

I suspect that if I had asked my informants, "Would you take *tiNDi* at so-and-so's house?" instead of whether they would take specific foods, the answers might have been more organized, and perhaps closer to actual practice.

We have discussed caste identities, distinctions, and ranking based on customary food practices. I shall now turn to the role of food and eating in relations between affines (in-laws), and between people and supernatural beings.

---

[10] Marriott (personal communication) has also indicated to me that he no longer considers it possible to determine a system of caste ranking on the basis of this type of data.

Chapter 8

CEREMONIAL FOOD EXCHANGE BETWEEN AFFINES

The relations between affines (in-laws) are characterized by formality and mutual respect. Persons whose children are married to each other (and who call each other *biigaru*) are cautious and restrained in their dealings with each other.[11] It is important to their relationship that gestures be made in the most proper manner possible.

As with other behavior toward affines, it is important that food exchanges should be done with proper respect for each other's dignity. Beginning with the wedding feast itself, foods provided for affines should be of high quality. If they are not served the best food available, at ceremonies or even during visits, affines may feel offended. Such feasting is part of the competitive aspect of their relations with each other.

The ethnographic literature on South India has amply demonstrated that throughout the domestic cycle of family development, there are many such events, which typically consist of people, gifts, and foods moving back and forth between the houses and villages of people who are related to each other by marriage. These data from Chinnapura further support that observation.

Pregnancy, Birth, and First Menstruation

There are some occasions when certain types of foods accompany gifts from one party to the other. One such exchange occurs during the seventh month of a woman's pregnancy--especially her first pregnancy--when she leaves her husband's house to go to her natal home

---

[11] This formality does not preclude friendship. Brothers-in-law, for example, are often friendly and visit each other frequently, if they live close to each other. But the possibility of discord is always present in any affinal tie.

for confinement. Though each caste has a slightly different practice, all observe this occasion with feasting and food exchange. A Washerman informant described sending his wife back to her father's house: she takes the elements of a meal with her, for cooking--coconut, a chicken (or, if rich, a goat or sheep), raw rice, and brown sugar. (She will not take salt with her.) Both families will eat together on this occasion. The husband's mother will bring a plate full of paddy, coconut, plantains, a bunch (one *kaT*) of betel leaves, flowers, and areca nut.

When the girl returns to her husband's house a few months after the birth, her natal family sends some side-dishes and snacks--*doose* "pancakes," pumpkin or eggplant *palya*, and sometimes *TamTa*, a sweet preparation consisting of balls made out of pounded soaked raw rice, brown sugar, dried coconut, fried Bengal gram, black sesame seeds, cardamoms, and ginger.

A Harijan informant told me that any time a girl is sent back to visit her mother's house, they must send *tiNDi* "snacks" with her. He also mentioned *doose* "pancakes" and the *tamTa* preparation. He stated that it is also necessary to return foods with the girl when she goes back to her husband's house.

A Smartha Brahmin informant stated that the girl going in her seventh month of pregnancy must go with her arms full of "five kinds of rice." These are flavored snacks prepared from cold boiled rice. They also appear at the bedding-down (first consummation) ceremony in a wedding and at a feast of the goddess Varamahalakshmi.

Another such occasion is that of a girl's first menstruation. I observed the exchange of *yecca*--twelve dried coconuts, brown sugar, fried Bengal gram, betel leaves, butter, one fresh coconut, bananas, nutmeg and cloves, a new sari and blouse piece--between two Harijan families on such an occasion. This combination of foodstuffs was brought to Chinnapura by a party from another village, who came to announce their daughter's first menstruation. And when the Chinnapura party returned to celebrate the event, they also took *yecca* to the girl. I was told that on this occasion it was the girl's mother's brother, mother's father, and mother's sister's husband that took (*y)ecca* to her.[12]

Marriage and the buvve shaastra *Ceremony*

The Hindu wedding in this region typically includes a ceremony specifically oriented toward food exchange and eating. During this ceremony, which is called the *buvve shaastra*, the bride and groom generally eat a meal together, and feed each other; and there may be ritualized food exchange or sharing between representatives of the bride's and groom's parties as well.

I have information on this ceremony for five castes (Fisherman, Barber, Washerman, Peasant, and Harijan/A.K.) from a combination of observation and informants' descriptions, observing it myself among Peasants and Harijans. I was not able to find out whether this ceremony is included as a part of a Brahmin wedding.

Before discussing the ceremonies themselves, I want to suggest that there are at least two different levels which may be considered. In the first place, the bride and groom eating together is an obvious metaphor for their sexual relationship, considering the close association between eating and sex in this society. Secondly, this meal is a metaphor for the joining of the two families, especially since the two groups of affines participate in the *buvve shaastra* ceremony[13].

The equation of food and sexuality is such common metaphorical coin, that it sometimes is difficult to tell which is primary and which is metaphorical. A member of the Washerman caste told me of a man who was outcasted because he was "taking food in a Barber house," that is, he had a Barber caste mistress, and was taking meals in her father's house. In another case, a woman who had apparently fallen into a life of prostitution was described as "taking food from any house at all." The statement about the food was certainly true, but it implied more.

In the Barber and Peasant caste versions of this ceremony, the people who actually partake of the food are not the bride and groom themselves, but other members of their respective groups, though the

---

[12] According to the Dravidian kinship system, these relatives all are structurally "affines" in relation to the girl, especially her mother's brother.

[13] The term *buvve* is a baby-talk word for food or boiled rice.

bride and groom are always there. One reason for this may be that the sexual metaphor in the bride and groom feeding each other is too strong. In doing the eating ritual in an indirect, group-oriented way, the signification reverts back to the thing that the bride and groom's commensality was symbolic of, namely the union of the families. The symbol could thus become clearer than it would be if obscured by the sexual overtones of the eating act.

Regarding the second level, there also are metaphors that have to do with the relations of the bride and groom as representatives of allied (intermarried) kin groups. For example, in some of the ceremonies the respective kin-groups eat the food that the bride or groom has left on the plate. This is true of the Harijan, Fisherman, and Washerman caste ceremonies, although in the Peasant caste ceremony there seems to be some crossing, with the opposite sides eating each other's food--though this is not a case of the actual left-overs being eaten. In the Peasant caste ceremony, the competitive relation of affinal groups is represented in a race to finish eating.

Different castes do *buvve shaastra* at different stages of the marriage. The Peasants and the Harijans observe this ceremony on the day after the wedding has taken place. After the bride has been taken to the groom's house (her future residence, according to patrilocal custom), the bride's family comes to take the couple back to the bride's house again on the next day. The ceremony of consummation of the marriage will not yet have taken place. The bride's family in both the Harijan and Peasant groups provides all the food. That is, they bring all the food for the ceremony with them, but the ceremony itself is done in the groom's house.

Fisherman caste families conduct this ceremony on the day after the wedding, according to informants. I assume, therefore, that it is probably done in the bride's house, where all the other wedding ceremonies will have taken place. In regard to the Washermen and the Barbers, I do not have any explicit statement about which day or in whose house it is done.

Customary **buvve shaastra** *Foods*

The meals shared in this ceremony contain the elements listed in Figures 9 and 10. Castes that include these preparations are indicated in parentheses.

FIGURE 9
Main Dishes for *buvve shaastra*

anna	boiled rice	(Fisherman)
huggianna	"hodgepodge" of boiled rice and vegetables	(Barber)
uggiboona*	mixture of boiled rice, brown sugar, ghee, and ripe banana	(Washerman, Peasant and Fisherman)
appaDiTTu	a mixture of brown sugar, cardamom, ginger, black sesame, ground together and mixed with doose "pancake" batter, and boiled and poured into a stone mould. Fried Bengal gram is pressed on outside.	(Harijan, Peasant)
naamdaalige	a boiled mixture of brown sugar and rice flour, which is poured into a metal plate and cooled, and cut into pieces. (Plate purified with cow urine first.)	(Fisherman, Harijan)

---

* boona, like anna, refers to boiled rice; huggianna and uggiboona, are therefore similar words with different referent.

FIGURE 10
Side Dishes and Condiments for *buvve shaastra*

taLDa		(Fisherman)
tarkaari gojju	vegetable gojju	(Peasant)
palya or gojju		(Barber)
hapLa	oil-fried pappadum	(Barber, Washerman, Peasant)
kajjaaya	a fried sweet	(Barber)
bella	brown sugar	(Harijan)
uppinkaayi	pickle	(Washerman, Barber)
tuppa	ghee (clarified butter)	(Harijan, Barber, Peasant)
baaLehaNNu or haNNu	ripe fruit, usually banana (baaLe=banana)	(Peasant, Barber, Harijan)
kaayi (tenginkaayi)	coconut	(Peasant)
baaLekaayi	green banana	(Fisherman)

Sequence of Events: buvve shaastra *Rituals*

The **Washerman ceremony** description I got is relatively simple. Briefly, what happens is that the bride and the groom sit together with two men of each of their families sitting with them, presumably on either side of the couple.[14] First the bride feeds the groom some food. Then the groom feeds the bride. And then the men from either side finish the food, according to my informant. The actual meaning of the bride's "feeding" the groom, or the men "finishing" the food in this case is not entirely clear, since we did not observe the ceremonies ourselves. For instance, the bride's "feeding" the groom--or *vice-versa*--could mean

---

[14] This is the only caste where we have a record of no women in the supporting parties.

either that she puts some of her food onto his plate, or that the bride and groom actually put food from their plates into each other's mouths. The fact that other relatives finish eating the food, however, makes it rather unlikely that they are actually feeding each other. If they did, then their "saliva" would be said to pollute their plates, and though there is a symbolic "saliva" pollution of the plates, for the two sets of supporting relatives, such real pollution is somewhat unlikely to occur.

The **Fisherman caste ceremony** description is similar to that of the Washerman caste, and the report is equally vague. The couple sits together. They exchange food from each other's plates. And after the exchange, the "best men" and "bridesmaids" eat the things. Then they throw out the remnants.

The *buvve shaastra* **among the Barbers** involves the following actions. The "bridesmaid" group mixes the food from the bride's plate into a ball and puts it into the bride's hand. She then feeds the groom. Then the "best men" put food into the groom's hand, and he then feeds it to the bride. This sequence is repeated three times. Then the two groups eat the remaining food, and the bride and groom together eat betel leaf and nut. They get up, and the ceremony is completed.

One Barber informant gave two distinct terms that I am translating as "best-men" and "bridesmaids": *aDaldamma* and *aDaldangi,* respectively.[15] Before any of the official wedding ceremonies begin the Barber bride and groom feed peeled banana to each other. This done just after the worship of sacred clay wedding pots (*araNe*),[16] which itself involves the offering of a meal ((*y)eDe,* or "offered meal") to the pots. A portion of that offered meal is taken out and reserved for the *buvve shaastra* meal. The *buvve shaastra* was described by my Barber informant with this necessary background information.

The Harijan sequence is somewhat more complicated than the Washerman and Barber rituals, possibly because I have more information on it. My information comes from two informants, and also from observation. The bride and groom have plates set in front of them. Food

---

[15] These terms are related to kinship terms: *tamma* = "younger brother," and *tangi* = "younger sister."

[16] All of the *marriage* ceremonies for which I have descriptions include preliminary offerings to these clay pots.

is put on those plates two times. After the first serving, the bride and groom are covered with a towel (perhaps while they eat). After both of these two servings, the bride and groom give their food to children. Then they are served a third time. The groom takes food off of his plate and puts it onto the bride's plate. Then apparently the girl's plate of food is eaten by the girl's side, and the boy's plate of food is eaten by the boy's side. (There is no mention here of the bride putting food back onto his plate, as is done by some other castes in this ceremony.) After this exchange, according to observational data, one half of the food that has been cooked is given to married women (*muuTayide*) of both sides, and the other half is given to other villagers.

One informant provided supplementary information on the Harijan ceremony. He said that the bride and groom eat what has been served to them, and the "brothers-in-law" of the boy and the "sisters-in-law" of the girl eat together in two groups. [*Editor's note:* Photo No. 20 below may show this activity, but the notes are not clear.]

In the case of **the Peasant caste ceremony**, my own observations and one informant's description supplement each other. It would have been difficult to understand this complex event without both. Before the ceremony was performed, when the bride's family first came to the groom's family house, two groups of "friends" – representing the two families -- brought with them two baskets. These baskets were opened after a worship (*puujaa*) to the sacred clay pots (*araNe*) had been made, soon after the arrival of the bride's party. One basket was observed to contain bananas, coconuts, and betel leaf and areca nut. The other one contained prepared food. The food was taken from the second basket. Some of it was put on a leaf plate. Then a leaf plate of food was placed in a basket. Now there was a basket and a plate. I was told at the time, "The plate is the boy's and the basket is the girl's." (All food had been provided by the girl's family.) The plate and basket apparently had no relation to the boy and girl themselves, but were designated in this way to represent each of their sides.

The Peasant bride and groom sit in front of the sacred clay pots (*araNe*) on a black blanket (*karikam-bligadde*). The "bridesmaids" and "best men" sit with them. The bride's elder sister and the groom's sister or his brother's wife bring two plates, put the food on the plates, and do a *puuja* "worship" for the plates which involves breaking coconuts.[17]

After worship has been done for the food on the bride's and groom's plates, the groom's elder sister was observed to switch the bride's and groom's plates back and forth three times. (There are sequences of thrice-repeated exchanges throughout these ceremonies. Another one is at the beginning of the wedding, when the bride and groom exchange garlands three times.)

Then the bride makes a ball of the food that is on her plate and puts that ball on the groom's plate. He then takes that ball and puts it on the floor. Then he does the same thing makes a ball of his food, puts it on the bride's plate, and she puts the ball of food on the floor. This sequence is repeated three times.

While the bride and groom are exchanging food balls, according to my informant, the two groups of "friends" on either side are eating food, which is called *buvve*, in competition, as described below. I did not observe this event, but it is a well-known part of Peasant weddings in the Chinnapura region. This competitive eating is one of the most interesting and distinctive features of the Peasants' *buvve shaastra* ritual.

After the bride and groom have eaten, a person in the category of "mother-in-law" (*atte*) from the bride's family was observed to give the groom one rupee. Then the bride's and groom's plates were given away, one to a member of each family.

Then the groom's elder sister put a peeled banana on each plate, broke it up, and moved the pieces back and forth from plate to plate. Then

---

[17] It is interesting to compare these two relatives (the bride's elder sister and the groom's sister or brother's wife), since they are mirror-images of each other in the two affinal groups. The bride's elder sister is inevitably married, because, of the rule of marrying off elder siblings before younger ones (that is, unless she is just a classificatory elder sister, in which case the rule would not apply). Therefore, she is a member of a different lineage than the bride herself. It is probably considered auspicious in this ceremony (as in many others) to have a married woman perform the ceremonial function. On the other hand, the groom's brother's wife or his (possibly unmarried) sister would be of the same lineage as the groom. It is possible of course that these two women might be of the same lineage as each other, and as the groom, in the event that there had been other girls from the bride's lineage given to the groom's lineage before the wedding being performed.

she washed both of their hands, first over the boy's plate and then over the girl's plate. That would mean, of course, that she poured water over their hands, and that the water drained into the plates.[18] She then gave the groom betel and nut, and he handed it to the girl. They got up, and this was the end of the ceremony as I observed it.

As soon as the metal plates of the bride and groom had been exchanged at the beginning of the ceremony, by the groom's elder sister, the basket was given to the party representing the boy's side, and the plate was given to the party representing the girl's side.

According to my informant, while the bride and groom are eating their food and doing the ceremony as described above, "they cover all, except the bride and groom, with a blanket, and they eat in competition."[19] Whichever party finishes first puts its hands (with "saliva" *injaLu* contamination from eating) onto the defeated party's plate. Then the defeated party also puts *injaLu* "left-overs" to the winning party, and they then throw everything away. Then all members present are served dinner.

Comparisons and Contrasts Among buvve shaastra *Ceremonies*

Since we are viewing these ritual events from a social structural point of view, rather than a purely descriptive one, it is necessary to move to another level of abstraction and identify some patterns in this material. I shall also briefly indicate what these ceremonies can tell us about relations between affinal groups, and about social structure in general. It is not possible to do an extensive analysis with these limited data, but it is possible to demonstrate that the patterns of food exchange are sociologically enlightening.

It is possible to distinguish at least three types of *buvve* shaastra ceremonies practiced among these five castes: (1) the Barber, Fisherman, Washerman; (2) the Harijan; and (3) the Peasant types.

---

[18] This action is similar to a part of the wedding called *dhaare,* in which members of the audience to the wedding pour water and milk over the bride's and groom's hands in sequence, as a sign of giving approval to the match.

[19] In one Harijan wedding I observed, during another part of the ceremony of the wedding, members of the groom's lineage, five young men, sat under a blanket and ate some rice from a common plate.

The Barber type of ceremony seems to indicate or establish equality between the two sides, a structural theme common to many of our caste ceremonies. According to our descriptions, these ceremonies are generally characterized by the bride and groom feeding each other (with help from the two supporting parties, at least in the Barber case), and then -- in the Fisherman and Washerman cases -- the two supporting parties finishing the food from the two plates.

The Harijan ceremony involves more different categories of people than the others, that is, in terms of who eats as part of the ceremony. These are: a) children, b) the boy's and girl's sides, c) married women from both sides together, d) the whole "village," which in the case of the Harijan Colony, is a single-caste settlement. These several categories do not appear as distinctively in the *buvve shaastras* of the other castes.

Another important contrast between the Harijan and other ceremonies is that in the Harijan case the first exchange that takes place is the boy giving food to the girl. For the other two groups on which my information is this specific, the girl gives food to the boy as the first move. The significance of this difference is not clear to me, considering that the pattern of relations between affines is generally similar among the castes. For example, the boy's party is the first to formally approach the girl's party during the period of marriage arrangement in all five groups. (Among the Brahmins of this region, the girl's side initiates marriage arrangements, and pays a dowry besides.) All of these five groups pay a nominal sum as "bride price," rather than paying a dowry.

One of the most interesting features of the Peasant ceremony has to do with the two groups of "friends" who eat food in competition as part of the event. Another distinctive element of the Peasant caste's *buvve shaastra* is the open competition between the two groups, this being a game-like form.

Though these ceremonies can be shown to symbolize the separateness of various categories of persons, they also symbolize union in a powerful metaphorical sense. By suggesting a mixture of *injaLu* "saliva" between the bride and groom, who symbolically eat each other's "left-overs," these ceremonies involve gestures of intimacy second only to sexual relations themselves. The act of sharing "left-overs" is probably the most intimate act possible for a man and woman to commit in public.

Chapter **9**

FOOD OFFERINGS TO SUPERNATURAL BEINGS AND ANIMALS

Gods, demons, and ancestors are fed on various ritual occasions during the Chinnapura year. It is interesting to consider the implications of this fact. People's comments and actions strongly suggest that these beings are perceived as members of this community or society in some sense -- as significant forces to be dealt with at certain times. Special foods are offered to supernatural beings of various types. Because of their widely discussed food preferences and the social importance of rituals for them, it makes sense to include them in this study of regional food practices.

In Mysore State [Karnataka] generally, the nucleated village can be viewed as a cluster of people in houses, the houses and villages being surrounded by evil spirits, especially at night time. Though this may seem dubious at first, such a belief does seem to limit people's movements out of their houses and beyond village boundaries during the night.

Regarding ancestors, as far as the residents of any particular house are concerned, the ancestors are somehow still functioning members of the family. Seeing ancestors as relatives who happen to be dead, rather than as ghosts or other evil spirits, brings us close to the view of Chinnapura residents on this subject. Since they are dead, they do not have bodies, but they are capable of being contacted; of communicating with others; and of being fed meals. As I have mentioned elsewhere, they are in fact fed annually by all castes. (This view of ancestors is common to China and Japan as well, as Newell (1968) has pointed out.)

As I explained in Chapter 3, there are several different types of gods, goddesses, and demons distinguished in this region. Whereas followers of other religions might differentiate gods and other spirits (such as ghosts) from each other, the Hindus seem to see them on a continuum that includes all beings, including humans and animals.

It might be useful to consider supernatural beings as another type of "caste," at least for some purposes. The term "caste" (or *jaati*) is applied to types of animals as well as to different categories of people. And it seems logical to include supernatural beings in this continuum, especially considering their presumed intimate relationships with living people. For our purposes, in discussing the system of food practices, this is especially convenient. In his article, "A Structural Definition of a Folk Deity of Tamil Nad," for example, Dumont discusses the relation between two deities in Tamilnad--a vegetarian god Aiyanar; and a meat-eating god Karuppu, who are *deevaru* and *deevate*, respectively. He sees the meat-eating worshippers of the two gods as defining their own roles in terms of the relationship between the two deities, master and servant. He argues that, "This structure of the divine needs to be considered in relation to the social order." (Dumont 1959:83)

One Brahmin informant described the set of non-Sanskritic village deities as "lower-order gods." Though we heard this as a somewhat agnostic statement at first, he was indicating accurately the view that a religious specialist can have of the different types of deities in the Hindu village system.

Different Gods' Food Preferences

Within the range of permissible types of foods for gods, some are thought to please certain gods more than others. As Dumont (1959) has pointed out, the non-vegetarian deities (*i.e.*, those who accept animal sacrifices) tend to have more power according to common belief. The most well-known of the Hassan District, Mysore, non-vegetarian deities is the goddess Maramma, who is assumed to have the power to inflict or cure smallpox, cholera, and other calamities on whole populations.

The contrast between the two major deities represented in Chinnapura raises some interesting possibilities regarding the symbolic value of their food preferences. The Brahmin priest in charge of the Narasimha temple (Narasimha being a major Sanskritic deity) told my wife that Narasimha had less power to protect the village than Maramma (the local South Indian "smallpox" goddess).[20] The reason given for Maramma's greater power was her preference for non-vegetarian food. The priest said that since she received offerings of chickens and other animal sacrifices, her power extended several miles beyond the boundaries of the village. Narasimha, on the other hand, only received offerings of curds, rice, and other vegetarian products, and therefore did not have as great a radius of potency as Maramma did.

This is on the surface an extremely deviant statement, since a distinction is ordinarily made between physical strength and spiritual strength. Meat is usually thought to give great physical strength, but vegetarianism results in spiritual strength. It is naturally to be expected that the strength of a god is spiritual.

In this particular case, the statement of the priest was equivalent to a metaphor of social reality. Although the Brahmins dominated the village of Chinnapura, the Peasants were dominant throughout the rest of the peninsula. The comparative strength of their respective gods is undoubtedly associated with this fact.

The elephant-headed god Ganesha is generally assumed to love *kaDabu*, a steamed preparation made of ground rice and black gram. Thus the god receives offerings of this food at the time of the Ganepathi festival, during which he is thought to visit all village homes. Similarly, the Lord Krishna is thought to adore *puri*, "puffed rice." In fact, most festivals are associated with specific foods, and are sometimes referred to by their food: "the *kaDabu* festival," "the *puri* festival," and so on.

A dangerous spiritual presence is represented by the lesser supernaturals called *devvas*. They are seen as extremely threatening, and their ubiquity after nightfall is acknowledged by educated and uneducated villagers alike. They usually limit their attacks to those travelling alone, but under certain circumstances are dangerous to anyone who comes near certain spots, or who crosses rivers, or who carries pork or beef with him. (A precautionary measure in the latter case is to wrap two chili peppers in with the meat.) The preferred food of *devvas*, judging from the terror they inspire, would seem to be human flesh. However, in

---

[20] Suzanne Hanchett, personal communication.

answer to questions about this, I seldom got agreement, although their interest in pork, beef, and animal blood was widely acknowledged.

Special meals are prepared for *devvas*. At village-wide festivals, offerings were commonly made to them before or after the festivities--at the non-Brahmin festivals *kuuLu* (rice soaked with blood) was offered. At the Brahmin-dominated *jaatra* festival mentioned above, the offering was rice colored with turmeric.

Ritual Purity as a Requirement for Making Food Offerings

It is important to note that in order to feed supernatural beings, a person must be in an extraordinary state of ritual purity. Once he or she has performed actions that make him/her ritually pure (*maDi*), an individual can usually offer cooked rice, meat, or other foods to most gods whom they desire to please, as appropriate. Though some of the deities found in the larger temples--*i.e.*, Sanskritic gods such as Narasimha--seem to require Brahmins to prepare food offerings, many gods can take cooked food from other castes as well.

Three examples from Chinnapura and Bandipur indicate that the ritual condition of purity or impurity of a house or lineage can also affect patterns of worship of a group's gods. In Bandipur there is a lineage in the *daas* Peasant group that has as its "house god" (*mane deevaru*) the goddess of wealth, Lakshmi. Worship is done for her on a weekly basis, and the various family heads of the lineage rotate this responsibility annually. However, at times when this lineage is subject to birth or death pollution, the goddess cannot accept offerings of food or other worship from members of the line. At the end of the eleven-day period of separation, the line calls in a Brahmin to remove *puruDu* or *sutaka* pollution from them, in order that they may resume worship of Lakshmi. (The Peasants actually use the term *sutaka* for both of these types of pollution.)

A similar relationship exists between the Lakshmi goddess of the Chinnapura Harijan Colony and the Colony itself. I was informed that the temple had become "polluted" with *sutaka* for the last year or so, and that it had been generally considered to be favored by one or another deity.

Foods <u>Not</u> Offered to Spiritual Beings

A few categories of foods are never offered to either gods or ancestors. One of these is salt, and the other category includes specific varieties of bananas. Informants of a wide range of castes have told me that salt is never placed in any ritual offering, even if whole meals must be prepared without any use of salt, as in the case with the Brahmin death-anniversary offering. Neither gods nor demons receive salted foods. There are several possible alternative explanations of this prohibition. One is that it may have an unfortunate association with the practice of throwing salt on a body which has been laid in the grave just before the body is covered with soil. Another interpretation that has occurred to me is that salt may be associated with things corporeal--ashes, human remains, the structure of the body itself. Since supernatural beings have no salty bodies, perhaps they are not thought to require salt for their food. The third possibility is that salt may be associated with loyalty. One non-Brahmin informant from another part of Mysore has told me that once a person has taken salt in someone else's house, one cannot ever betray him. Professor Moni Nag (in a personal communication) has suggested to me that this is a Muslim belief that has filtered into South India from the northern parts of the subcontinent.

At least twelve different varieties of banana are grown and used in the Chinnapura region. But six of these are considered unacceptable as offerings to deities. The Kannada names of the unacceptable varieties are *maarabaaLe, kaLanbaaLe, kalyaaNabaaLe* (very large), *buuTbaaLe, kaTbaaLe*, and *candrabaaLe* (red) and *ragaTabaaLe* (red). I do not know why these are forbidden as offerings, but the information was confirmed by questioning of four different informants in Chinnapura. The red color of the last two may somehow disqualify them.

Though deities have preferences and dislikes, in common belief, their worshippers also do. Just as there are vegetarian and non-vegetarian castes, there are also vegetarian and non-vegetarian deities; these parallels will be discussed further in the following chapter.

Receiving prasaad *After a Food Offering*

As I have mentioned above, foods and other things, such as flowers, offered to supernatural beings are generally distributed among propitiants as *prasaad.* This is considered to be that which is left over after the deity has used up the essence of the offering. At times there is competition or even fighting over receipt of *prasaad*. (One party may feel that they did not get enough, or that *prasaad* was not distributed to them in proper order.) In Chinnapura there is a dramatic and interesting case of *prasaad* distribution. Every procession for the goddess Maramma that goes around the village stops at the home of the *jooDidaar* (former landlord of the whole village, who is also the *patel* "head man" of the village) for a ceremony called *iiDakaayi*, literally, "throwing the coconut." The *jooDidaar* stands on the steps of his house and holds a coconut high above his head in one hand. As the crowd waits eagerly, he throws the coconut down on the ground as hard as he can, splitting it into many fragments. After he has done this, children in the crowd dive for the fragments, scrambling and pushing each other, in order to get as many as they can. They are playing, but they are also fighting for the joint blessings of the *jooDidaar* and Maramma.

Distributions of *prasaad* generally involve only half of the foods that the propitiant sponsor provides for the worship. The rest of the offered foods are given to the priest who performs the ceremony. Thus, if a coconut is offered to the deity, and an official priest (generally Brahmin, but possibly another caste) performs the *puuja* "worship," the priest will keep half of the coconut and distribute the other half in pieces to the audience participants. In larger-scale ceremonies, the priest may actually acquire a substantial amount of fruit, vegetables, and raw rice by this means.

Feeding Demons and Buffalo Sacrifice in a Maramma Festival

Some acts of worship to the goddess Maramma involve food offerings. Before a large Maramma *jaatra* festival in Chinnapura, food is carried to feed the demons that surround the village, presumably so that they will not interfere with the main part of the ceremony. This food is called *kuuLu*, and in this case it consists of rice soaked in blood. A goat is killed, and all the goat blood is gathered and kept in a pot. This blood is mixed with cooked rice, which is intended for three kinds of *devvas*: "demons," called *rakshasa,* "demons" called *durgi*, and "imps" called *piiDe*. The man who carries the *kuuLu* preparation "loses his senses," as they say. He goes into trance. Five other men hold him. Each of them has a stick. A Harijan of Chinnapura, named Dyavayya, generally has this duty. The five others wave their sticks over his head to keep the ghosts away. They carry the food, and the Harijan band comes. They circle the Harijan Colony, and put the food in some government land which was given to the Colony. (They claim that it must not be put anywhere else.) They then return to the Colony and bathe, subsequently performing *puuja* worship for a toddy pot called *gate*. They will then carry five toddy pots to Maramma, putting them in a line outside her temple. Kept inside the temple is her idol: a wooden figure with a silver face and silver hands and feet.

Description by informants of the subsequent buffalo sacrifice is as follows. The buffalo (*i.e.*, male buffalo, called *kooNa*) will be brought in front of the temple to a stone called *bali kallu* "sacrificial stone." They will tie it there and cut its head off. The head of the buffalo is kept near the toddy pots. On the head they put one red millet ball (*raagi hiTTu*). On that they keep a clay dish called *sarabi*. The rest of the body is cut up, and the suet is kept on this dish. They cut off one of the front legs of the buffalo and put it in the mouth of the buffalo's head. (This is a common part of such sacrifices, as described by Whitehead (1927) and others.) They then make a fire in the fat. Before this they will have brought water from the river and put it in front of the plate, so that the fat will float in the water while burning.

Only the Harijans eat buffalo meat. But after the Harijans cook the meat of the sacrificial animal, the Peasants go and watch them eat it, to ensure that it is done properly. The Harijans drink toddy, eat the meat, and then they dance. After this, the man who earlier carried the rice and blood offering comes forward, and the buffalo head is placed on his head.

The next day, in the morning, villagers of other castes will sacrifice goats and chickens with the help of Washerman priests (*puujaaris*), who lay out other things for the worship, such as coconuts, fruits, camphor, flowers, and red powder (*kumkum*). The animals themselves must, however, be cut by Harijans. The food which is thus provided, including meat, cooked rice, millet balls, and *saaru* "soup/curry," is divided as follows: half goes to the Harijans, and the other half is divided among the Barber (musicians), Washerman (priest), and Fisherman (village assistant, *talavaara*) functionaries.

The male buffalo will have been purchased with contributions collected by a group of Harijans from all village houses. Even Brahmin houses contribute to this fund. There need not be only one buffalo sacrificed on this occasion. According to my informants, separate families may make vows to Maramma throughout the year that if their buffaloes have male calves, the first one will be kept for sacrifice to Maramma. There may be as many as twenty or fifty male buffaloes killed in front of the temple, and all heads will be treated in the same way.

The head of the buffalo is considered to be a god. The man who carried the *kuuLu* (someone of Dyavayya's family, or Dyavayya himself) will again carry this head. The man will "lose his senses" again. The procession, with a Harijan band, will leave the Chinnapura area and go near to another village. They will choose one tree--some *haaladamara* (a tree with a milk-like sap)--and put the sacred buffalo head under the tree in front of an image of the god. They perform *puuja* "worship" there, and after the *puuja* return to Chinnapura. They will then bring all the silver ornaments for the image back to the *jooDidaar's* house for safekeeping. Members of the Madiga caste (leather-workers) will be waiting near the tree to take the head away to cook it.

Unfortunately, I was unable to observe this ceremony while residing in Chinnapura, but these detailed reports from multiple informants serve to demonstrate the important role of food and feeding in the Maramma festival, as a unifying event for the village.

Pig Sacrifice to Maramma

A slightly different description of a Maramma pig sacrifice was given to me by an informant from Bandipur. The group that is organizing the sacrifice collects raw rice and finger millet flour from all village houses. A leaf canopy (*pandal*) is erected near the Maramma shrine. Washerman priests will do worship, or *puuja*, and then the pig to be sacrificed is brought to the shrine. They cook the rice, make balls of the millet flour, and feed these items to the pig. This was called "putting *kuuLu*" to the pig. Only members of the Washerman caste group sacrifice and eat the pig. This feast is not a *jaatra* type of festival similar to the one described for Chinnapura, but a more limited event. It does demonstrate, however, the intimate role between the Washerman caste and Maramma in this region, and the type of cooperation between castes that characterizes worship of this goddess.

Pig Sacrifice and Other Offerings to Byadaramma/Mastiamma

The goddess Byadaramma (or Mastiamma) is represented in numerous small stone shrines distributed over the fields of this region. According to informants, this goddess is actually a type of *devva*, "ghost or demon," which can harm a whole lineage. The spirit is generally assumed to be the ghost of a woman who was killed or injured by a predecessor of a specific lineage.

Typically, something may go wrong in the lineage, and the family goes to a seer, who tells them that the trouble is due to the fact that some deceased relative murdered a woman long ago. He will tell them that the trouble will only be relieved if they put up a shrine and worship Byadaramma every year. The Divali Festival (*diipaavali* in Kannada) seems to be a common occasion for this type of worship in both Chinnapura and Bandipur. One Washerman informant of Chinnapura, however, is expected to go together with his whole lineage (*daayaadi* or *aNNatammandiru*, literally "brothers") to sacrifice a pig every year after the New Year festival, *uugaaDi*. The shrine in this case is a rock grown into a tree.

Though Byadaramma takes a pig, the male who shares the shrine with her (named *byadru*) takes chicken sacrifices. This informant told me that Byadaramma ruled this area before the Palegars did.

Perhaps because of the ghostly quality of Byadaramma, one informant told me that the Divali Festival offering (*yeDe*) to her is "like a funeral meal or ancestral offering (*tiiti*)." The menu dictated to me for this meal was cooked rice, millet balls, *palya* made of squash (*savrekaayi*), bitter gourd (*hagalakaayi*), and eggplant (*muulaayi*); meat *saaru*; and sweet *paaysa*.

Flower Offering to a Ghost

Another, similar type of offering is made in the event that a person feels he has been fear-struck by ghosts, though this offering does not involve the offering of cooked rice or a full *uuTa* meal. A small statue is erected out of mud, and a flower called *kaNigal huuvu*[21] is offered to the statue, together with "three colors of rice," one colored with turmeric, one with the red *kumkum* powder, and one with charcoal. This flower is

---

[21] *Nerium indicum*, oleander

also put on the head of a dead person during his or her funeral, according to some informants. This ceremony is performed either by a priest (*pujaari*) of the Washerman caste, or by a Vishnuvostamba Aynoru of a nearby village called Somavara.

Vegetable Sacrifice

A vegetarian worshipper may perform an act equivalent to animal sacrifice, to either a vegetarian or non-vegetarian god, by using vegetables defined as equivalents of animals. In Brahmin ritual one type of squash called *budgumbalakaayi* (ash gourd) can be substituted for an animal and sacrificed to a god. The procedure is to bore a hole in the squash, fill the hole with the red powder called *kumkum*, so that the inside of the squash has a red color, and then to chop the squash in half as if a blood sacrifice were being performed. Apparently a green lime can also be sacrificed as if it were an animal in Brahmin ritual. Both substitutions are thought to provide all the benefits of animal sacrifice with none of the defiling disadvantages of being associated with death. (Animal sacrifice, though frequent, is legally prohibited).

Offering Food to Animals

A few animal species are fed ceremonially. The sacredness of cattle is well attested. Ritual feeding of cows is practiced on a number of occasions.

A more spectacular feeding of animals is seen at the feeding of cobras. Cobras are seen as animals of high caste. They wear the *naama* or u-shaped caste mark of Vishnu on their heads, and also are sacred to the god Siva, whose image wears a cobra around the neck. Cobras are worshipped by barren women, who offer them milk; and they are honored with a festival, *naagarapancami*. The termite hills that dot the area are thought to be their homes, and milk and ghee are poured into them.[22] A Bandipur Smith caste neighbor family of ours was honored to discover that a cobra had made its home in the rafters of their house, and they offered it milk daily.

---

[22] Hanchett's book, *Coloured Rice* (1988/2022), includes detailed descriptions and analyses of this festival and of Hindu ancestor worship ceremonies in the same region.

The term *bali* refers to offerings of part of the food thrown out for the consumption of supernaturals before dining outdoors on ritual occasions. It is usually consumed by dogs. During the village wide ceremony (*jaatra*) in Bandipur, *pongal*, a rice and gram mixture, was deposited at various locations in the village for the feeding of supernaturals, as I have described elsewhere. (The name of the deity whose duty it was to provide food, through the agency of the priest and his assistant, was *balideevaru*.) It was expected in this case that the food would actually be eaten by dogs.

A third level of feeding animals is the feeding of crows, animals of extremely inauspicious aspect. Crows are, of course, carrion eaters. Crows are also fed offerings after ancestor ceremonies. The ceremonies are not complete until their appearance.

Feeding the Ancestors

The annual or death-anniversary offering to ancestors always involves giving them a meal. Non-Brahmins and Harjans observe this ceremony annually as *maaladahabba* or *pitra paksha*, usually around the time of the Dessara holiday. Brahmins do the full ceremony at the time of the death anniversaries of their parents, but they also make a general offering to ancestors on the day that other castes do their ancestor ceremony.

These events are organized in a very complex pattern, which generally stresses the themes of commensality and gift-giving between the ancestors of each family. In the Brahmin case, the ceremony on the death anniversary involves inviting two or three other, non-lineally related Brahmins to impersonate the ancestors being propitiated. These guests eat the offered meals on their behalf.

The foods offered by non-vegetarian castes to their ancestors always include meat preparations. The Brahmins include a preparation made from black gram called *uddinvaDe*. Because of the association between this preparation and this ceremony, Brahmins of this region seem not to prepare it in their homes, even though it is a popular snack in restaurants and coffee shops throughout the state.

A Fisherman informant told me that members of his caste should eat fish at the time of the ancestor ceremony, and also for the festival of their patron goddess, Ganga.

A Peasant caste informant told me that during this ceremony milk and meat are eaten together, because things that should not be mixed together are mixed during an inauspicious ritual.

Feeding Spirits and Social Redistribution of Foods

In the next chapter I shall discuss the symbolic value of such "mixing," as possibly referring to the mixture of living and dead persons in the lineage together. Among Brahmins, it seems, rice balls are thrown on the roof of each house, to be eaten by crows, which are thought to represent the ancestors themselves. These balls are called *hinde*, a cognate of the well-known Sanskrit term *pinda*, "rice ball." This is done at the conclusion of the ceremonial offering in the house.

In conclusion, I wish to discuss the feeding of the gods as "imaginary" parts of the local system of redistribution of foodstuffs. Feeding gods and demons is similar to the use of the square root of -1 in engineering. That is, it has meaning, even though it refers to a non-existent quantity. In the case of the square root of -1, it is possible to work out perfectly real quantities by using it as an intermediary term in problem solving.

In the case of gods and other spiritual beings, actual movements of persons and exchanges of foods are effected through the use of these conceptual devices; it is possible that the imaginary parts of the social system force these movements into the shape that they have. In a sense, the presumed social "reality" of these supernatural entities is the product of the action of other, more visible social forces–a way of legitimizing the social actions and exchanges required by rituals.

These supernatural elements of the social system are one medium that refracts a certain amount of real wealth being sent in the direction of other humans:

1) The major portion of it goes to the groups and individuals who serve as priests to the gods; and

2) A part of it is redistributed as *prasaad* to poor individuals, and therefore functions as a sort of rudimentary social welfare device.

A strict materialist might say that the only important fact here is that the gods never really eat, that only people (and some animals) eat, that foods actually move in the direction of priestly groups as a result of these beliefs. From a sociological point of view, however, it is important to point out that if this particular symbolic system were not available, then these foods might never reach those destinations, and even if they did, the movement would not be as smooth as it seems to be.

Obviously these social functions could be arranged without the mythological element, or the mythology could be manipulated to different social arrangements. And to some extent the supernatural tribute system has been obsolesced by private land ownership by individuals. Ritual redistribution can also be replaced by secular welfare systems, and this development is also evident, especially at the regional level though less so in villages.

Illustrations

Maps

1– 2. Maps of India

Map 2. 2017 Map of India, Showing Karnataka State

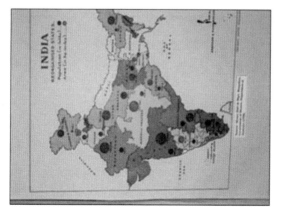

Map 1. 1958 Map of India, Showing Location of Mysore State (Karnataka)

3a-3b. Karnataka State

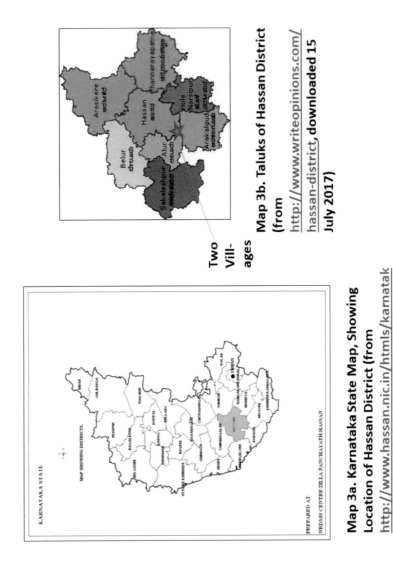

Map 3b. Taluks of Hassan District (from http://www.writeopinions.com/hassan-district, downloaded 15 July 2017)

Map 3a. Karnataka State Map, Showing Location of Hassan District (from http://www.hassan.nic.in/htmls/karnataka_map.htm, downloaded 15 July 2017)

4a-4b. Chinnapura and Bandipur villages

MAP 4b. BANDIPUR VILLAGE

Bandipur is approximately two miles west of Chinnapura, across the Hemavati River, in Hassan District, Hassan Taluk.

MAP 4a. CHINNAPURA VILLAGE

Chinnapura is located on a peninsula formed by the confluence of the Yagachi and Hemavati rivers, in Hassan District, Alur Taluk.

Source: Superintendent of Survey, Settlement, and Land Records (Bangalore, 1967)

Photos

1. Crossing the River

1. CROSSING THE RIVER FROM THE MAINLAND TO THE PENINSULA

Traveling across the river, from the mainland to the peninsula

2. Village Scenes

Old village gate, Chinnapura 1967

Chinnapura street scene (photo by Doranne Jacobson, International Images)

Tree at village entrance (above)

3. Village Wells

3. VILLAGE WELLS, USED FOR DRINKING WATER

4. 'Dry Lands' and 'Wet Lands'

Fertile red loam, typical of Hassan District

Replanting rice seedlings on wet lands, Bandipur 1966

A.K. woman plowing her own land, Chinnapura 1967

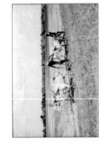

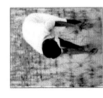

5. Planting in Dry Land

5. PLANTING IN DRY LANDS

6. Harvesting and Processing *Raagi*

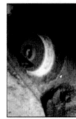

Stones for grinding *raagi* (finger millet) in village kitchens

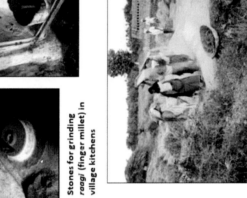

Winnowing grain

Harvest scene

Threshing floor

7. Fishing

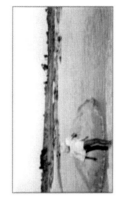

Net fishing

7. FISHING

ng: dividing the catch

Basket for catching fish

8. Pigs and Goats

8. Pigs & Goats

Local pigs (above), sold at Hassan market (below)

9. The Cherished Oxen

10. Brahmin Families

10. BRAHMIN FAMILIES, AND BRAHMIN GIRLS COLLECTING WATER

11. Non-Brahmins

A Village leader

Typical women's saris

11. NON-BRAHMINS

A Peasant caste family

12. Residents of the Chinnapura A.K. Colony

13. Verandahs

Brahmin house (less wealthy) with simpler verandah

13. VERANDAHS

Adjacent houses of two wealthy *jodidaar* brothers with elaborate verandahs

Moderate- to low-income households with simple verandahs (above and right)

14. Decorated Home Entrances

Servant applying *rangoli* to a Brahmin family's verandah for a special occasion, Bandipur 1967

14. DECORATED HOME ENTRANCES

Home entrance (threshold and verandah) decorated with *rangoli* line drawings and flowers

15. Kitchens

15. KITCHENS

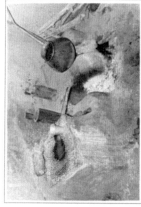

A.K. kitchen (above) with wood burning stove, fuel, bamboo measuring cups, other items

Non-Brahmin kitchens with wood burning stove & fuel (below), covered drinking water pot (left), and other items

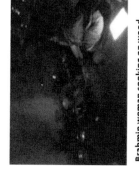

Brahmin woman cooking on wood burning stoves decorated with *rangoli*

Brahmin kitchen with large shrine (above)

Festival cooking (left)

16. Making Butter

16. MAKING BUTTER IN THE HOME

17. Pounding Grain

17. POUNDING GRAIN TO MAKE FLOUR

Pounding grain during an A.K. wedding ceremony

Pounding grain in a village kitchen

18. Washing Kitchen Vessels and Utensils

18. WASHING KITCHEN VESSELS AND UTENSILS AT THE RIVER: A DAILY CHINNAPURA ROUTINE

19. Two Auspicious Rites of Passage

Weaver caste wedding, Bandipur 1967

Girl's first menstruation ceremony (Bandipur Peasant – left / below & Chinnapura A.K.- above, right)

19. TWO AUSPICIOUS RITES OF PASSAGE

20. Eating Food During a Wedding Ceremony

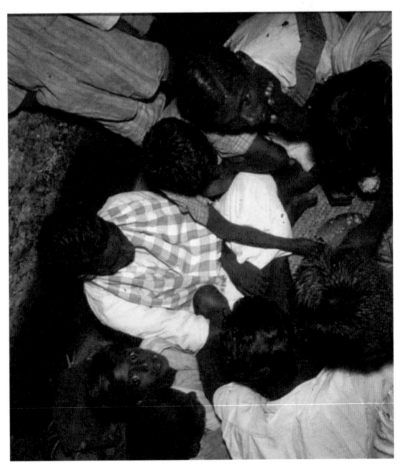

Wedding party participants eating food from a common plate (Chinnapura, A.K. Colony, 1967)

21. *aaraNe* Vessels in Wedding Ceremonies

Peasant caste wedding, Chinnapura

21. *AARANE* VESSELS (ANCESTRAL WITNESSES) IN WEDDING CEREMONIES

Shepherd caste wedding, Chinnapura

A.K. wedding, Chinnapura

22. Shrines and Deities-1

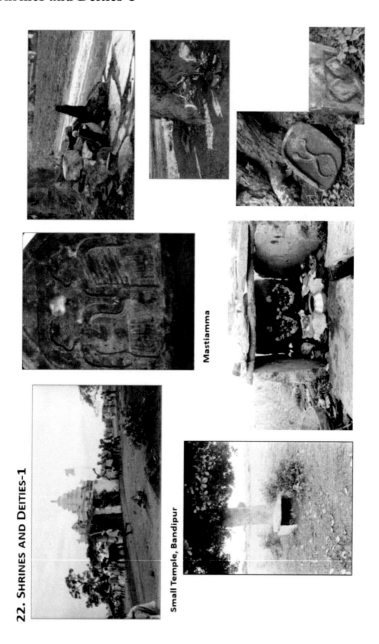

22. SHRINES AND DEITIES-1

Mastiamma

Small Temple, Bandipur

23. Shrines and Deities-2

23. SHRINES AND DEITIES-2

Structure (*pandal*) near river, used for performance of various types of ceremonies (above and right)

24. Cooking Outdoors in a State of Extreme Purity

Preparing in advance of the holiday

Outdoor stoves built for the occasion

24. COOKING OUTDOORS IN A STATE OF EXTREME PURITY FOR THE NAGPANCAMI HOLIDAY

Cooks dressed in white have bathed and are fasting

25. Food Offerings-1

Fisherman caste woman offering foods at a small shrine in the center of Chinnapura, during the Dipavali (Divali) holiday. She collects donations from all households, prepares the food, and distributes offered foods as *prasaad* to children after completing her offering. (1967)

Food offerings to goddess Maramma during a holiday in her honor in the A.K. Colony (Bandipur village, 1967)

26. Food Offerings-2

Ceremonial offerings before a wedding (above). The pot may represent the ancestors.

Barber caste family's annual offering at an outdoor shrine to goddess Mastiamma, followed by a *puja* to their house goddess, Lakshmi, in the form of three pots, called *kalasas*. (Chinnapura, October 7, 1967)

26. FOOD OFFERINGS-2

27. Feeding Male and Female Ancestors

Chinnapura, 1967

28. Feasts

People of similar social status eat sitting side-by-side.

Funeral feast after death of the father of a prosperous Peasant caste man, Chinnapura region, 1967, with *raagi* balls for the guests (above)

Wedding feast, hosted by a Chinnapura Peasant caste family, 1967 (above)

29. Religious Specialists: Brahmins and Others

29. RELIGIOUS SPECIALISTS: BRAHMINS (TOP ROW) AND OTHERS (BOTTOM ROW)

Vaishnava Brahmin Priest

Maramma Temple: a group of families rotate priestly responsibilities

Siva Linga Temple

Pujaari at A.K. Wedding

Yoganarasimhaswamy Temple

Dasayya at 28-village Jaatra

30. A.K. Musicians

Groups of musicians are available for weddings and all other ceremonial occasions. This is a specialty of the A.K. community.

31. Personal Photos

Stanley Regelson and Suzanne Hanchett, 1967

G.S. Gopal Setty, Stanley Regelson, Suzanne Hanchett

Stanley Regelson and a Peasant caste friend

Stanley Regelson with A.G. George

32. Some of Our Research Assistants

Left to right: K. Gurulingaiah, P. Rangaraju, Malla Setty, Stanley Regelson, H. Bettaiah

Left to right: K. Gurulingaiah, H. Bettaiah, Malla Setty, P. Rangaraju, Stanley Regelson, Suzanne Hanchett, P. Jayamma

33. Disappearance of a Village and Its Environs

Irrigation dam at Bandipur Village (right), and the water
submerging Chinnapura and the surrounding peninsula
(above), 1976

House Diagrams

1. A Peasant Caste House

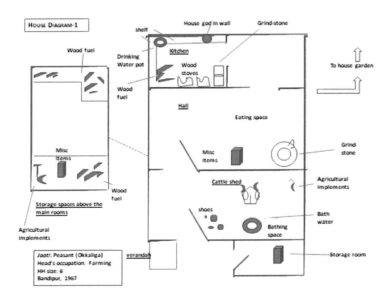

2. A Smith Caste House

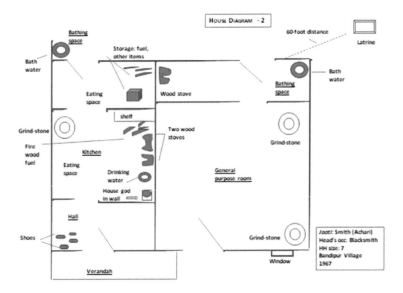

3. A Washerman Caste House

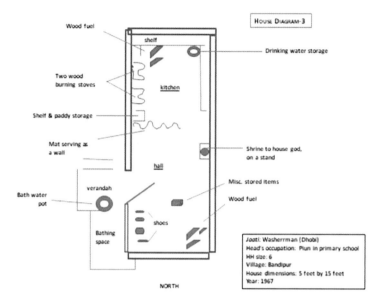

House Diagram-3

Wood fuel

shelf

Drinking water storage

Two wood burning stoves

kitchen

Shelf & paddy storage

Mat serving as a wall

hall

Shrine to house god, on a stand

Misc. stored items

verandah

Wood fuel

Bath water pot

Bathing space

shoes

Jaati: Washerrman (Dhobi)
Head's occupation: Piun in primary school
HH size: 6
Village: Bandipur
House dimensions: 5 feet by 15 feet
Year: 1967

NORTH

10

CULTURAL ISOMORPHY AND FOOD SYMBOLISM

The folk science of individual and group character (*guNa*) in Chinnapura rests on theories of food and speciation. These are built up as relatively "arbitrary" symbolic systems (as defined above in Chapter 2) within certain nutritional and ecological limits. And they have application to the everyday world of social behavior at several levels.

Beyond nutrition and ecology, there is another kind of limitation on the use of food as communication in social life. This is an overriding set of culturally defined structural distinctions that penetrate many aspects of village life. These patterns constitute what anthropologists call the "world view," "cosmology," or basic "themes" in South Indian and localized culture. Whatever term is used to label them, they consist of a simple set of distinctions and rules which can be applied in a wide variety of settings in the Hindu world.

Now that we have inspected the social setting of Chinnapura and introduced some of the most socially and culturally important aspects of food behavior, we are in a position to discuss the "structural implications" of this behavior. By this I mean, parallels among different cultural domains. The isomorphies we seek are not always simply synchronic relations between domains, but can cross temporal, spatial, and social boundaries. For instance, I once asked a father whether he was going to arrange his son's marriage with an "old relation" (a family already connected by marriage ties) or a new house. The father metaphorically compared the two types of marriage arrangement with ordinary food and festival food:

1

old relative	new relative
ordinary food (nickatle)	festival food (heckatle)

In itself, this metaphor suggests certain attitudes. But it also indicates that certain other contrasts might be similarly patterned. This is a simple case of isomorphy across domains (food and kinship), but insofar as it reflects a relationship between two sets of relationships, we can speak of "structure."

This type of isomorphy between domains is not the only type we must deal with. Dumont, for example, refers to the fact that in certain places in India, the expected isomorphies may differ in content, while retaining the same patterns. For instance, in most places, the pattern is essentially: Brahmin/non-Brahmin, vegetarian/non-vegetarian:

2

Brahmin	non-Brahmin
vegetarian	nonvegetarian

Structural variation also may manifest itself along temporal or other dimensions. For instance, at several times in my questioning, I was told that different types of food produced different types of character. One of these groupings I have already mentioned. It is the one that represents the characteristic foods of the three caste levels in Chinnapura: vegetarian, non-vegetarian, and beef-eating.

3

vegetarian	nonvegetarian	beef

But, from Brahmins familiar with the scriptures, I usually got a more archaic answer:

4

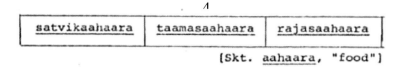

satvikaahaara	taamasaahaara	rajasaahaara

[Skt. aahaara, "food"]

These three represent, respectively, mild food; spicy and luxurious food; and a diet of meat and liquor.

I also elicited the following set, which, I was told, distinguished between the life of action; the life of intellect; and the life of the rustic peasant, respectively:

5

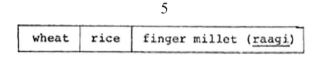

wheat	rice	finger millet (raagi)

Furthermore, a fourth set occasionally came up:

6

rice	finger millet (raagi)	sorghum (jooLa)

Maize and sorghum are both called *jooLa* in Chinnapura. Neither was in wide use twenty years ago. Both are increasingly used--maize with the introduction of hybrid corn, and sorghum with influence from North Mysore District (formerly part of Bombay Presidency), where it is an important food crop. No one in Chinnapura eats *jooLa* who can possibly afford rice or finger millet, however.

Now, as far as most people (non-Brahmins) in Chinnapura are concerned, the set labeled 4 is unknown. It is a relic; or perhaps it refers to North India, where "twice-born" caste members are subject to various degrees of voluntary austerity.

Set 5 is also a relic, this time, more obviously, of a period when this part of South India was dominated by bread-eating Muslims and Englishmen. I was startled to hear the person I was interviewing that wheat was somehow "highest," and I suspected flattery on the part of my informant. He did in fact remind me that I was a wheat-eater.

The set marked 6 is the one associated with class rather than caste. The three grains are in the order of descending price, and no one eats much of the grain above his own economic level. It is very likely that this is a descriptive set that will become more prominent in the future.

Curiously, each of these sets calls forth a description of a three-level society, even though in each case the contents are different. Those in 3 are caste levels. Those in 4 are levels of refinement. Those in 5 reveal a mixture of ethnic and social groups, defined by their food habits. And those in 6 are economic classes. The persistence of the three-part set (or "trichotomous theme," as Saraf, 1970 puts it) is striking.

Basic Structuring Principles

Some distinctions are needed to interpret the data presented in the preceding chapters. Two especially important ones are: (1) the "cold"/"hot"/"neutral" quality distinction; and (2) male/female/*muTTu* (*muTTu* being "menstruating woman"). Several authors have discussed such classificatory patterns for Indian cultural systems and for other societies. Numerous possible applications to our food data are raised by these discussions. When applied to food items (or other types of items, such as medicines) in alternate combinations, such basic distinctions are useful in interpreting possible meanings of choices at a symbolic level.

Rather than serving as an inventory of cultural facts, or a set of simple instructions on filing or classifying cultural items, such distinctions as these serve to provide patterning in relationships between elements. Classification of foods into "hot" and "cold" categories, for example, vary from one individual to another, but each person does make such a classification, based on the common assumption that "hot" and "cold" things affect health and well-being. Violations of categorical taboos do not alter the patterns themselves. Consider the case of one Peasant, headman of his hamlet, who is required to eat beef one day a year, in order to propitiate the spirit of a murdered Harijan. He retains his social position despite violating a food taboo.[23]

---

[23] Marriott (1959) argues that it is important to record variation as we observe it, and I agree. But consideration of more abstract cultural patterns is also a valid endeavor.

"Cold/"Hot"/Neutral. It should be mentioned that in general sweet foods are cooling and pungent foods heating. This casts an interesting light on the fact that *siihi*, "sweet" and *kaara*, "peppery," are habitually used as metaphors for vegetarian and non-vegetarian food, respectively:

7

siihi	kaara
non-meat	meat

Non-meat *vs.* meat suggests this correspondence, which is also generally (though not consistently) accepted:

8

non-meat	meat
cooling	heating

This leads to the possibility of:

9

+ semen	menstrual blood
cooling foods	heating foods

Certain foods are considered to be excessively heating, or *caraku*, "burning." This fact suggests the following set of distinctions:

10

coolness	heat	excessive heat

Excessive heat is considered to be actively dangerous, and menstrual discharge is thought to be excessively heating. (One informant mentioned that it is dangerous to the eyes, to have sexual intercourse with a menstruating woman. Care of the eyes requires coolness, as demonstrated by the practice of offering burning camphor to gods, "to cool their eyes.") It is possible, then, to continue with:

11

coolness	heat	excessive heat
semen	menstrual blood	menstrual discharge

This suggests a further association between excessive heat and the color black. (In our Western apprehension of colors, the logic of cool white, hot red, and burnt black seems logical. Whether this is also logical in this form to Hindu cognition is still a matter of speculation.) Brenda Beck (1969) makes a convincing case for the systematic relation of South Indian color distinctions to the "hot"/"cold" system of food values, white and green being cooling, red and black being heating. She may be pointing towards a double-bipartite scheme of the following order; though she does not present her findings in this manner:

12

	Cooling	Heating
Male	white	black
Female	green	red

Such a description, if it is cognitively accurate, may articulate with a tripartite scheme without either structure being invalid.

Male/Female/*muTTu*. Regarding the third basic distinction, there is a connection in symbolic terms between sexual and purity distinctions. A woman in her menses is a special kind of human being, and the extreme attention drawn to the menstruating condition in South Indian custom has the effect of making it visible to the point of raising it to a level equal with the distinction between the two sexes itself. Harper (1964) describes a three-level system of pollution among Kannada-speaking Havik Brahmins: *maDi* "pure," *mayLige* "impure," and *muTTuceTTu* "untouchably polluted." The latter state (called simply *muTTu* in Hassan District Kannada) is generally viewed as that characterizing menstruating women and Harijans. The word *muTTuceTTu* is unknown in Chinnapura, but the generally recognized concept of extreme pollution corresponds to Harper's descriptions.[24]

Traditional Hindu and local Chinnapura physiology alike see conception as the result of the union of semen and menstrual blood. They appear to be equal elements:

13

male	female
semen	menstrual blood

One value of over-arching schemes of basic distinctions to the study of foods is that they provide a basis on which we can interpret the "meanings" of manipulation of particular food items in ceremonial or other contexts. Though I have not emphasized this aspect of the study, I would like to indicate some possibilities by use of a few examples. These examples have to do with the use of clarified butter (ghee), fruits, turmeric, turmeric mixed with lime, black gram, black sesame, and brown sugar in rites of passage and ancestor ceremonies.

Anthropologically, the statement that the generative principle is the link between the individual ego and the structure of the external world would seem to be a statement about kinship. In the Brahmin, death-anniversary ancestor feast, one important element in the offered meal is ghee. Those persons representing the ancestors on this occasion are stuffed as full of ghee as they can possible be. This stuffing is a part of a meal in which they are forced to eat as much as they possibly can of many different foods, but ghee is especially important, according to my informants. If our symbolic interpretation based on color and other qualities is correct, the worshippers are in effect bestowing fertility (or, more exactly, semen) on their own line by this offering. In a sense they

---

[24] Harper draws attention to the fact that the Havik Brahmins' three degrees of purity/pollution correspond to the three large social groupings in South Indian social structure -- Brahmins, non-Brahmins, and Harijans -- and also to the three orders of supernaturals - *deevaru*, *deevate*, and *devva*.

are building semen in the ancestor to whom the offering is made, and in themselves as his descendants.

There is frequently another level in this ceremony, that is, a level at which affines are involved in exchange. For the persons chosen to represent the ancestors in this ceremony are often affines of the lineage performing the ceremony. Since members of the lineage are forbidden to perform the role of the ancestor, wives' brothers and other close affines are commonly called for this purpose.

As I mentioned above, one Peasant caste informant told me that meat and milk are eaten together during the ancestor-propitiation ceremony, because things that should not be mixed are mixed during an inauspicious ceremony. One symbolic referent of such mixing may be the mixing between the living and the dead of a family or lineage. This ceremony – as performed by all castes -- does emphasize unity through commensality, but the unification must be done carefully, because there is some danger to the living on an occasion that brings them near to deceased people.

On the "hot"/"cold" continuum, many "black" items are also thought to be physiologically "heating," if ingested. Several informants indicated that brown sugar (jaggery, *bella* in Kannada) is considered to be heating; and one informant explained that although brown sugar and peanuts are both heating, their combination has a total effect of cooling. Black sesame is considered to be excessively heating.

The Brahmins use black sesame in monthly and annual ancestor-propitiation. They also use black gram (*uddu*) as a basic element in death-anniversary ceremonies. As a result, I was told, no Brahmin should eat the popular *uddin vaDe* restaurant snack, unless he has already lost a close relative. (This is reminiscent of the Jewish custom of having children leave the synagogue when the prayer for the dead is recited.)

Such associations may constrain the symbolic uses of foods. That is, it is possible that once a food is used in a particular context (such as an inauspicious ceremony, associated in some way with death or funerals), a food may take on some of the meanings associated with that inauspicious context, thus becoming unacceptable for use in auspicious occasions. Thus, the delicious black sesame sweets may not be considered suitable to wedding feasts because of their association with less auspicious events, although other types of sweets figure prominently at weddings. However, one ceremony in which black sesame figures prominently is the ceremony performed for a newly menstruating girl in the Iyengar Brahmin group. In Chinnapura and Bandipur, Iyengars distribute huge sweet balls made from black sesame and brown sugar when a daughter matures.

This schematic approach also raises some interesting questions about the symbolic value of brown sugar, which is an important ingredient in some of the ceremonies that have been discussed throughout this book: the *buvve shaastra* and the ceremonies for the newly menstruating girl. Since the Hindu wedding traditionally preceded this latter ceremony in earlier days of child marriage, but was consummated only after the bride matured, the two situations are traditionally related.

This opens the way for a translation of sorts, an interpretation of the meanings of using this particular food rather than some other food. The girl is being lost to her ancestral lineage, and the reference to the dead is connected with this. In the ceremonies associated with first menstruation, brown sugar is an essential component of the *(y)ecca* assortment of foods carried back and forth among relevant categories of relatives, especially among non-Brahmins and Harijans.

In the *buvve shaastra* wedding ceremony of eating together, described in some detail above in Chapter 6, brown sugar is brought (together with other elements of the meal) to the groom's house by members of the bride's party after the wedding has been completed. During the *buvve shaastra* event, as I described it above, the couple eats together, exchanges foods, and usually there are other exchanges made that involve representatives of the two newly-related affinal groups.

To focus on brown sugar, however, I would like to suggest the following implications of using it, by extending symbolically from the distinctions that have been presented here. When two lineages are joined through marriage, the character of the lineage is defined ancestrally in this ceremony. Deceased members of the lineage are not considered to be absent simply because they are dead. Rather, they are considered to play an active role in all family events, to be actually present in a sense. If brown sugar is identified as being "black" in color, and if "black" represents death as a state of being, it might be possible to conclude that the food itself (the brown sugar) is a substitute for the ancestors, and that the participants are symbolically ingesting each others' ancestors, or at least, ingesting each other's lineages, ancestrally defined.

The statement that would be symbolically made by this act is that the exchange represented by marriage is of profound importance. The alliance resulting from marriage is so deep that one could say that one set of ancestors is allied to another set of ancestors once a marriage has taken place between two lines.

Brown sugar and black sesame balls are, incidentally, considered to be very "heating," to the point of actually endangering health by causing bloody dysentery.

Ritual Substitutions

The practice of ritually substituting some foods for others has been noted at various points throughout this study. A satisfactory general scheme of distinctions may ultimately provide a guide to such substitutions. It may be that there are sets of items which share most important characteristics, and which can therefore be used as alternatives by different groups, in feeding deities or ancestors, or in other rituals. One might say, for example, that black gram functions similarly to meat; that blood and turmeric are functionally similar; that milk or clarified butter are used by Brahmins in ways that some other "white" and "cooling" substance (such as buttermilk) are used by non-Brahmins. There may also be a pair of mutually substitutable "green" items, perhaps including bananas and areca flowers.

The food-and-character *jaati* system and the cosmic system of basic distinctions can be said to intersect in the following paradigm, which identifies major classes of beings according to their feeding patterns. These three can be separated into three levels, according to three grades of auspiciousness:

FIGURE 11
Structural Paradigm of Foods and Types of Beings

	Vegetarian	Nonvegetarian	Eaters of unclean flesh (human or carrion)
Supernaturals	deevaru (Sanskritic deity)	deevate (Local deity)	devva (Minor spirit)
Castes	Brahmins	non-Brahmins	Harijans
Animal Species	Cobras Cattle	Dogs	Crows

Celestial Bodies and Purity/Pollution

The association of the sun and moon with male and female principles in Hindu symbolism is widely recognized (Walker 1968). The importance of the eclipse (*grahaNa*) as a third type of major condition, neither night nor day but severely polluting is clear, at least in the practices of local Brahmins. All cooked food that is in the house during an eclipse must be disposed of. Exceptions can be made if twigs of the sacred *tulsi* (*Ocymum sanctum*, or sacred basil) plant are placed on pot lids, but except for preserves or pickles, few will flirt this closely with pollution (*mayLige*). Immediately on completion of an eclipse in Chinnapura, all the Brahmins purified their houses and went to the river to bathe. I was told that the event was the equivalent of every house being entered by a Harijan or a menstruating woman (*muTTu*).

Non-Brahmins, however, did not observe these measures. In fact, during an eclipse that took place just before the elections in 1967, the local non-Brahmin candidates held a political meeting in the certainty that no Brahmin would attend. Non-Brahmins nonetheless do observe precautions such as keeping pregnant women indoors during an eclipse, lest their infants be marked.

All levels of society, on the other hand, do respect *raavukaaLa*, a two-hour time span occurring every day of the week at a different hour. The period is named for the planet *raahu*, who is considered to be the monster responsible for devouring the heavenly bodies during an eclipse. During this daily period, which is marked on local calendars, no work of any importance will be done.

Two- and Three-part Paradigms

Following Saraf (1970), Harper (1964), and others, I have emphasized the apparent tripartite nature of certain social and symbolic structures. Alan Dundes (1968) has discussed three-part items in American folklore in a similar manner. Though Saraf is dealing mainly with Sanskrit sources, and Harper's and my material is from a region where a Dravidian language is spoken, this material does indicate that a "trinitarianizing" tendency is present in the sociocultural life of greater India.

Returning to Harper's three degrees of supernaturals, it is noteworthy that the foods of the three groups (*i.e.*, appropriate sacrifices or foods that they seek) differ:

14

deevaru	deevate	devva
(Sanskritic gods)	(local gods)	(demons)
vegetarian food	nonvegetarian food	pork and human flesh

The *devvas'* taste in human flesh is of course the essence of their danger. Pork is known to attract *devvas*, and precautions must be taken when one is carrying it, namely, inserting two black peppercorns in the package with the meat. Pig sacrifices are suitable for demons, and Whitehead (1921) presents evidence that human sacrifices were previously offered to *cavdis* (see discussion of feeding various categories of gods, Chapter 9) and other types of *devva*.

One reason the pervasiveness of these repeated trichotomies does not jump forward in many other interpretations is the visibility of apparent binaries. I suggest that the two-part schemes that are presented as the only interpretation of Hindu symbolic structures are results of excessive reliance on Brahmin informants. The Brahmin point of view dominates European scholarship in South India. My Brahmin informants tended to explain to me that there were only two types of human beings:

15

Brahmins	Shudras

Furthermore, there were only two types of supernatural beings:

16

Vedic gods	demons

Maramma, foremost of the *deevates*, is referred to as a demon-goddess by Brahmins as a result. It is not surprising, then, that we hear so often of paired qualities: male/female, hot/cold, right/left. I suggest that even so "obvious" a dichotomy as this may be part of a three-part scheme, since in fact the right/left distinction is considered important only in the upper half of the body; whereas the entire lower half of the body, particularly the feet, represents an exceedingly high degree of inauspiciousness. We can thus posit the set:

17

right hand	left hand	feet

Eating and giving to others must be done with the right hand. The left hand is reserved for polluting activities, like washing the anus after defecation. It is impolite to hand someone anything with the left hand. The feet are so unclean that it is bad manners even to point one's feet at another person. And to touch another person with one's feet requires an elaborate stylized apology. The most extreme form of giving respect and expressing deference involves touching someone's feet. One form of blessing practiced at temples involves touching of the devotee's head with an instrument representing the feet of the god.

I am suggesting that the Brahmin two-part understanding of the social structure leads to a different cosmological view than that of those who recognize a three-part social structure[25]. However, the patterns presented here are not elements in a single structure. Rather, they are components in a system that is continually manipulated; the following four characteristics of this system indicate that it is constantly changing according to a complex calculus:

1) Although the sets are isomorphic, they are not identical. Thus, an individual may be a Brahmin (first column) and a woman (second column) simultaneously. Yet in many cases, reference to one set may be symbolically substituted for another, as in Dumont's discussion of the relation of the gods to their worshippers.

2) Each element in the set is usually itself a continuum, even though the elements themselves are separated by quantum jumps.

3) Although many of these sets seemed fixed and inert, we know from the trichotomies presented at the start of the chapter that the contents are themselves freely subject to alteration when it is required.

4) As my informants said about the effect of "heating" and "cooling" foods on the body, sometimes the effect depends on the special characteristics of the individual. That is to say, the accumulation of different configurations in any situation places a variant interpretation of any new material to be added.

Changes in ecology, demography, outside influences, and other forces continually tend to alter society, keeping these elements in a state of constant change. It is my conviction that food is the medium in which even the subtlest changes in structure can be indicated. I have tried to indicate some cases in which this was fairly well documented. It is clear, however, that much work remains to be done to fully understand issues of structure in the Hindu village setting.

---

[25] This conforms with the view of Durkheim and Mauss in *Primitive Classification* (1963).

Chapter 11

CONCLUSIONS

This report so far has been a completely "emic" discussion of food language and practice in a Kannada-speaking village. That is, we have considered only the insider's point of view -- that of people sharing a common cultural framework. Some rules of behavior within that cultural framework have been identified. But, as these findings demonstrate, individuals' adherence to their rules is not rigidly uniform. Rather, people tend to have differing interpretations of shared concepts.

In the preceding chapter, I considered the domain of food as a system of classification in itself, with relationships isomorphic to other domains within Kannada society and culture. For example, food sharing serves as a metaphor for the union of two families marriage and as a metaphor for sexual connection. And not taking certain foods from other castes clearly represents concepts of group distinctions and ranking.

The next step is to move in an "etic" direction, toward a scheme for cross-cultural comparison. As Lévi-Strauss has tried to demonstrate, "...The whole of human history may be looked upon...as a series of attempts to organize differently the same means, but always to answer the same questions" (1963:10) Like kinship categories, culturally-based food notions may have some regular patterns of variation. The Dravidian kinship system, for example, is not unique. Rather, its ways of classifying relatives – *e.g.*, some kinds of cousins (parallel cousins) as "sisters" or "brothers," not marriageable, and other cousins (cross-cousins) as potential mates -- are essentially the same as those of the so-called Iroquois system, developed by a number of different tribal peoples with otherwise very different social institutions. The normal, linguistically defined distinctions between lineal/collateral relatives, sex of relative, generation, and so on are similar, despite wide historical and civilizational differences.

The anthropological and other literature on food has yet to identify universally defined components that combine and recombine in socially or culturally meaningful ways, though there are many ethnographic reports on variations in food ideas and eating practices. This study is a move in the comparative direction. We have discussed the qualities attributed to foods in one place at one time: raw/cooked, physiologically "heating"/"cooling," meats/dairy/grains and seeds, fruits/vegetables, flavors (sweet, pungent/spicy, sour, bitter, astringent), and so on. How many other flavors are identified by human communities, and what are their semantic connotations (meanings) elsewhere? There is abundant anecdotal information on temperaments associated with flavors (sweet = loveable, for example, or sour = hard to get along with) but not much systematic analysis. Is meat-eating associated with strength in many other places, as it is in Chinnapura? Do others used sexual lust metaphors similar to the English, 'I *hunger* for your love'?

It is important to understand that the Indian perception of caste, as we view it, is linked to a cultural interpretation of animal speciation. That is, though the castes are defined in cultural terms (by services they exchange with each other), Hindus also conceive of the differences between castes as sharing the same characteristics as the differences between animal species. That is, Hindu folk zoology sees the defining characteristic responsible for the differences between species (jaatis) as the different "natural foods" of each species. The defining characteristic of each caste is seen in the same way.

Furthermore, the characteristics among these "natural foods" can be seen to form a pattern in themselves - that is, a system of patterned identities and distinctions. This pattern seems to provide support for the system of social units of which it is a part.

There is much cultural variation in associations between commensality, kinship, sexuality, and gender. One interesting point of variation is whether groups that do or do not eat together can or cannot marry each other's members. In some places, one can eat together only with people they also can marry: for example, in the Trobriand Islands. Among some totemic peoples, however, marital partners are found only among groups that do not share meals, and whose food taboos differ. Sexual contact and eating together also can vary. Among the Melanesian Lesu group, studied by the anthropologist Hortense Powdermaker, for example, it is possible to have sexual partners to whom one is not married; but one cannot eat together with them. (Powdermaker 1933) Among the Marri Baluch tribe of Pakistan, men eat with other men, and women, with other women. (Pehrson 1966) The only women men can eat with are those defined as "sisters."

Within one geographical area there can be different food customs, just as there are different dialects of a language or other cultural sub-divisions. Indeed, one study of Yiddish dialects in northern Poland found that exactly the same sub-cultural line divided two different pronunciations of the word 'to be' and two ways of cooking the popular *gefiltefish* (with or without sugar). (Herzog 1965)

An important food distinction in the northern parts of the South Asian subcontinent is *pakka* vs. *kacca*. Marriott (1959) describes the North India categories, *pakka-kacca-jutha* -- in which *pakka* represents food fried in fat, *kacca*, boiled food, and *jutha*, left-overs (symbolically or actually soiled by saliva). In this system *kacca* foods are those normally shared with caste-mates but not accepted from or shared with social inferiors. These distinctions do not have the over-arching power in the South Indian area covered in this study, although *jutha* is a close equivalent to the Kannada term *injaaLu* (literally saliva, including left-over foods polluted by another person's saliva).

In "The Culinary Triangle" (1966), Lévi-Strauss suggests a universal distinction in food processing that has a possible connection to the North Indian series. He discussed the categories moving from raw to roasted to boiled. If *pakka* is seen as the equivalent of roasted, a prediction by Lévi-Strauss takes on an interesting aspect: "...[T]he boiled can most often be ascribed to what might be called an 'endo-cuisine', prepared for domestic use, destined to a small closed group, while the roasted belongs to 'exo-cuisine', that which one offers to guests." In fact, one often is able to offer *pakka* foods to outsiders without making or implying any statement about social rank, while *kacca* foods are reserved for family meals (or offerings to social inferiors). Lévi-Strauss does not extend his scheme to the degree of human processing implied by *jutha*, or another person's polluted left-overs.

In a later work, Marriott (1968:142) added feces to the series as a possible fifth item. His justification of this was related to caste practices in North India, but the logic of Lévi-Strauss's position would actually require it as the ultimate in human (although not cultural) processing.

"Purity" and "pollution" concepts also are found among diverse cultures, of course, with India making the relatively unique connection between these ideas and the caste system. The Hindu kitchen is the innermost center of the home, one entered only by the closest associates. Protection of family purity and preventing offense to house-protecting deities enshrined in the kitchen justify this practice. Observant Jews hold the view that ingesting certain foods, or taking any food whatsoever in a non-kosher home would produce spiritually harmful "pollution" to a person, although most details of traditional Jewish cuisine and concepts of acceptable foods differ greatly from those of Hindus. In both cases distinct groups separate themselves from others, especially in settings where food is involved, justifying this separation by the fear of becoming polluted or otherwise harmed by the "other" group.

Culturally based food classification generally relates to popular classification of animals. And every known cultural system distinguishes between edible and inedible animals and demeans those who eat the animals that others consider inedible – as, in the Indian case, other Hindus look down on Harijans/Dalits for eating beef and carrion. In Western society we use derogatory terms for other ethnic groups that refer to their food habits: French people referred to as "frogs," or Germans as "krauts," for example.

Fasting is one culturally widespread food practice with widespread, well-studied symbolic overtones. Buddhists, Jains, Christians, Jews, and shamans of diverse groups all connect fasting with spiritual discipline, devotion, building special powers, and strength of character. The universal religions, most of which address fasting, all have something to say about food in general. Fasting is enhances spiritual purity; eating fish is better than eating meat; and so on.

Exchange is symbolically important in all known cultures. Gift-giving is the most easily observed, universal form of exchange. But marriage – sometimes spoken of as the gift of a bride – is also a form of exchange between patrilineal groups. Similarly, giving and taking of different categories of food is one way that social status similarities or differences are reproduced and affirmed in Hindu society. Feudal lords in Europe received tribute from their serfs in the form of raw foods. They reciprocated by giving feasts to their social inferiors. The lords provided other processed goods as well: manufactured items, such as clothing or armor. The giving of raw materials defined the social position of serfs, just as the giving of cooked or processed things defined the position of feudal lords.

The caste system is the social setting for this study of food customs. Hindu castes are culturally distinguished groups with a natural, immutable, hereditary association with specific occupations – a cultural "overlay" on nature. In the traditional *jajmani* arrangement, castes exchange services, but they are endogamous: they <u>do not</u> exchange women in marriage. Different clans or lineages within each caste do exchange women: *i.e.*, they are exogamous. The caste type of social order is the opposite of a totemic system in which "natural" species are associated with human groups. For example, Australian clans associate themselves with plants and animals, whose production they claim to control. These clans are exogamous: *i.e.*, they do exchange women.

Caste and totemism differ, then, in two key respects, as Lévi-Strauss (1963b) has argued: (1) Totemism involves exchange of women in marriage, while castes are normally endogamous units. (2) Caste involves a real exchange of services, while totemism involves an imaginary exchange of services – e.g., causing the increase of the totem plant, animal, or other natural item.

Other caste-like systems have been found in the Middle East, where some endogamous ethnic groups are associated with traditional occupations. Social life – especially organization of "racial" groups -- in the U.S. south also has been characterized as a caste-like system. These social arrangements, however, do not have the elaborate ritual overlay that is found in South Asia. They represent entirely different patterns of exchange.

In brief, exchange of food and sharing of food in human society are always symbolically significant; but what they mean differs greatly from one cultural group to another. Linguistically defined categories are all-important. Social, religious, economic, and political institutions are organized around such sharing and exchange in a dazzling spectrum of cultural possibilities.

BIBLIOGRAPHY

Aykroyd, W. R.

    1966 The Nutritive Value of Indian Foods and the Planning of Satisfactory Diets. New Delhi: Indian Council of Medical Research Special Report Series, No. 42.

Beals, Alan R.

    1962 Gopalpur: A South Indian Village. New York: Holt Rinehart and Winston.

Beck, Brenda E. F.

    1969 Colour and Heat in South Indian Ritual. Man, The Journal of the Royal Anthropological Institute 4: 4:553-572. (n.s.)

Beidelman, Thomas O.

    1959 A Comparative Analysis of the Jajmani System. Monographs of the Association for Asian Studies, No. VIII.

Berlin, Brent, and Paul Kay

    1970 Basic Color Terms: Their Universality and Evolution. Los Angeles and Berkeley: The University of California Press.

Beteille, Andre

    1966 Caste, Class, and Power. Bombay: Oxford University Press.

Bhutiani, R. C, ed.

    1963 Balanced Diets and Nutritive Value of Common Recipes. Compiled by M. Swaminathan, Kantha Joseph, M. Narayana Rao, S.V. Chandiramani, Bhutiani, R. C. Lalitha Subramanian, and K. Indira. Mysore: Central Food Technological Research Institute.

Bright, Jane O., and William Bright

1965 Semantic Structures in Northwestern California and the Sapir-Whorf Hypothesis. American Anthropologist 67:5, part 2, 249-258.

Bright, William

1958 An Outline of Colloquial Kannada. Poona: Deccan College Postgraduate and Research Institute, Poona. Deccan College Monograph Series, 22.

Carman, John B., and Frédérique Apffel-Marglin, eds.

1985 Purity and Auspiciousness in Indian Society (International Studies in Sociology and Social Anthropology, No. 43). Leiden: E.J. Brill.

Chomsky, Noam, and Morris Halle

1968 The Sound Pattern of English. New York: Harper and Row.

Conklin, Harold C.

1955 Hanunoo Color Categories. Southwestern Journal of Anthropology 11: 339-344.

1962 Lexicographical Treatment of Folk Taxonomies. *In* Problems in Lexicography. Fred W. Householder and Sol Saporta, editors. International Journal of American Linguistics 28:2, Part IV, pp. 119-141.

Counihan, Carole, and Penny Van Esterik, eds.

1997 Food and Culture; A Reader. NY and London: Routledge.

Douglas, Mary

1966 Purity and Danger. London: Routledge and Kegan Paul.

1972 Deciphering a Meal. Daedalus 101:1:61-81.

Dubois, Jean Antoine

1906 Hindu Manners, Customs, and Ceremonies. Henry K Beauchamp, editor. Third edition. Oxford: Clarendon Press.

Dumont, Louis

    1957a Hierarchy and Marriage Alliance in South Indian Kinship. Occasional Papers of the Royal Anthropological Institute of Great Britain and Ireland, No. 12.

    1957b *Une sous-caste de l'Inde du sud; organisation sociale et religion de Pramalai Kallar*. Paris: Mouton et Cie.

    1959 A Structural Definition of a Folk Deity of Tamil Nad: Aiyanar, the Lord. Contributions to Indian Sociology. Paris: Mouton and Co., No. III. pp. 75-87.

    1970 Homo Hierarchicus: the Caste System and its Implications. Julian Pitt-Rivers and Ernest Gellner, editors. Chicago: University of Chicago Press.

Dundes, Allan, ed.

    1968 Every Man His Way: Readings in Cultural Anthropology. Englewood Cliffs, New Jersey: Prentice Hall.

Durkheim, Emile, and Marcel Mauss

    1963 Primitive Classification. Rodney Needham, editor. Chicago: University of Chicago Press.

Emeneau, M. B.

    1967 Dravidian Linguistics, Ethnology and Folktales: Collected Papers. Annamalai University, Linguistics Department, publication 8. Annamalainagari.

Firth, Raymond

    1973 Food Symbolism in a Pre-industrial Society. Chapter 7, *In* Symbols; Public and Private. Ithaca, NY: Cornell University Press.

Frake, Charles O.

    1964 Notes on Queries in Ethnography. American Anthropologist 66:3, Part 2, 132-145.

Franklin, Karl J.

    1996 K. L. Pike on Etic vs. Emic: A Review and Interview. Downloaded from http://www-

01.sil.org/klp/karlintv.htm?mindsparktb_222529105res
ources%2Farchives%2F1562=&_ga=GA1.2.15365484
9.1499031342&_gid=GA1.2.1437488342.1499031343
(July 2, 2017)

Ghosh, Manomohan

1950 Natyasastra. Calcutta: Royal Society of Bengal.

Goodenough, Ward H.

1956 Componential Analysis and the Study of Meaning.
Language 32:195-216.

Gough, Eleanor Kathleen

1960 Caste in a Tanjore Village. *In* Aspects of Caste in South
India, Ceylon, and Northwest Pakistan. E. R. Leach, ed.
Cambridge: University Press. pp. 11-60.

Hanchett, Suzanne

1972 Festivals and Social Relations in a Mysore Village;
Mechanics of Two Processions. Economic and Political
Weekly VII, Nos. 31-33, pp. 1517-1522.

1974 Reflections and Oppositions: On Structuralism. *In*
Structural Approaches to South India Studies, Harry M.
Buck and Glenn E. Yocum, eds. Chambersburg, PA:
Wilson Press. pp. 5-16.

1976 Hindu Potlatches: Ceremonial Reciprocity and Prestige
in Karnataka. *In* Competition and Modernization in
South Asia, Helen E. Ullrich, ed. New Delhi: Abhinav
Publications. pp. 27-59.

1976 Land Tenure and Social Change in a Mysore Village. *In*
Aspects of Changing India; Studies in Honour of Prof.
G.S. Ghurye, S. Devadas Pillai, ed. Bombay: Popular
Prakashan. pp. 181-188.

1988 Coloured Rice; Symbolic Structure in Hindu Family
Festivals. Delhi: Hindustan Publishing Corp.

2003 Death Rituals; Life Cycle Rituals; Puberty Rituals. *In*
South Asian Folklore; An Encyclopedia, edited by
Margaret A. Mills, Peter J. Claus, and Sarah Diamond.

New York & London: Routledge. pp. 144; 354-358; 492-493.

2022 Coloured Rice; Symbolic Structure in Hindu Family Festivals. Pasadena: Development Resources Press, second edition. [e-book available at www.devresbooks.com and Amazon.com]

n.d. Symbolic Uses of Plants in Folk Traditions: A South India Ethnobotany Study.

Hanchett, Suzanne, and Leslie Casale

1976 The Theory of Transitional Phenomena and Cultural Symbols. Contemporary Psychoanalysis 12:4:496-507.

Hanchett, Suzanne, Tofazzel Hossain Monju, Kazi Rozana Akhter, and Anwar Islam

2014 Water Culture in South Asia; Bangladesh Perspectives. Pasadena, CA: Development Resources Press.

Harper, Edward B.

1959 The Hindu Village Pantheon. The Southwestern Journal of Anthropology 15:227-234.

1961 Cultural Factors in Food Consumption: an Example from India. Economic Botany 15:4: 289-295.

1964 Ritual Pollution as an Integration of Caste and Religion. *In* Religion in South Asia, Edward B. Harper, editor. Seattle: University of Washington Press,. pp. 151-196.

Hayavadana Rao C., ed.

1930 Mysore Gazeteer; Compiled for Government. Bangalore: Government Press, new edition.

Headland, Thomas, Kenneth Pike, and Marvin Harris, eds.

1990 Emics and Etics: The Insider/Outsider Debate. Newbury Park, CA: Sage Publications.

Hockett, Charles

1960 The Origin of Speech. Scientific American 203:3:88-96.

Iswaran, Karigoudar

1968 Shivapur: A South Indian Village. London: Routledge and Kegan Paul.

Karve, Irawati

1965 Kinship Organization in India. Bombay: Asia Publishing House, second edition.

Katcher, Joan Hall

1963 Semen Loss: Persistence of a Theme in Indian Tradition. Unpublished paper presented to the annual meetings of the American Anthropological Association: San Francisco, California.

Katona-Apte, Judit

1969 Food and Acculturation. Mimeographed paper presented at the annual meetings of the American Anthropological Association: New Orleans, Louisiana.

Kittel, Ferdinand

1894 A Kannada-English Dictionary. Mangalore: Basel Mission Book and Tract Depository.

Krishnappa, B.

1921 *Paka saustra*. Mysore: The government Branch Press, tenth edition. (In Kannada)

Lehrer, Adrienne

1969 Semantic Cuisine. Journal of Linguistics 5:1:39-55 (London: Cambridge University Press).

Lévi-Strauss, Claude

1963a Structural Anthropology. New York, London: Basic Books.

1963b The Bear and the Barber. Journal of the Royal Anthropological Institute of Great Britain and Ireland 93:1-11.

1966a The Culinary Triangle. New Society 22: 937-940.

1966b The Savage Mind. Chicago: University of Chicago Press.

1969 The Raw and the Cooked: An Introduction to a Science of Mythology, Volume I. New York: Harper and Row.

MacCormack, William

    1959 The Form of Communication in Virasaiva Religion. *In* Traditional India: Structure and Change. Milton Singer, ed. Philadelphia: Publications of the American Folklore Society, Bibliographical series, volume X.

MacCormack, William, and M. G. Krishnamurthi

    1966 Kannada: A Cultural Introduction to the Spoken Styles of the Language. Madison: The University of Wisconsin Press.

Marglin, Frédérique

    1985 Wives of the God-King: The Rituals of the Devadasis of Puri. Oxford University Press.

    2011 Subversive Spiritualities: How Rituals Enact the World. New York: Oxford University Press.

Marriott, McKim

    1959 Interactional and Attributional Theories of Caste Ranking. Man in India 39:2:92-107.

    1968 Caste Ranking and Food Transactions. In Structure and Change in Indian Society. Milton Singer and Bernard S. Cohn, editors. Viking Fund Publications in Anthropology 47:133-172.

Mauss, Marcel (Ian Cunnison, trans.)

    1967 The Gift; Forms and Functions of Exchange in Archaic Societies. New York: W.W. Norton & Company, Inc.

Mead, Margaret

    1964 Food Habits Research: Problems of the 1960's. Washington, D.C.: National Academy of Sciences, National Research Council.

McCutcheon, Russell T.

    1999 Theoretical Background: Insides, Outsides, and The Scholar of Religion. In The Insider/Outsider Problem in the Study of Religion, Russell T. McCutcheon, ed. London: Cassell Academic. Downloaded from http://www2.kenyon.edu/Depts/Religion/Fac/Adler/Rel

n101/McCutcheon%20-%20emic-etic.htm (July 2, 2017)

Mintz, Sidney W.

1996 Tasting Food, Tasting Freedom; Excursions into Eating, Culture and the Past. Boston: Beacon Press.

Moody, D.

1965 Chemotherapeutic Consequences of Culture Collisions. Proceedings of the Royal Anthropological Institute, pp. 33-45.

National Research Council

1943 The Problem of Changing Food Habits: Report of the Committee on Food Habits. Bulletin of the National Research Council.

1945 Manual for the Study of Food Habits: Report of the Committee on Food Habits. Bulletin of the National Research Council, No III.

Nayak, H. M.

1967 Kannada: Literary and Colloquial: a Study of Two Styles. Mysore: Rao and Raghavan.

Newell, W. H.

1968 Some Comparative Features of Chinese and Japanese Ancestor Worship. VIII International Congress and Ethnological Sciences. In Proceedings, of Anthropological Volume III, 300-301.

Om Prakash

1961 Food and Drinks in Ancient India, from Earliest Times to c. 1200 A.D. Delhi: Munshi Ram Manohar Lal.

Pehrson, Robert N.

1966 The Social Organization of the Marri Baluch, compiled and analyzed from his notes and with a preface by Frederick Barth. Viking Fund Publications in Anthropology, No. 43. Chicago: Aldine Publishing Co.

Pike, Kenneth L.

1954 Language in Relation to a Unified Theory of the Structure of Human Behavior, Part 1. Glendale, Calif.: Summer Institute of Linguistics. 170 pp. [Preliminary ed.]

1967 Language in Relation to a Unified Theory of the Structure of Human Behavior. Janua Linguarum Series Maior XXIV. The Hague, Paris: Mouton and Co., second edition.

Powdermaker, Hortense

1933 Life in Lesu: The Study of a Melanesian Society in New Ireland. London: Williams & Norgate.

Regelson, Stanley

1981 The Bagel: Symbol and Ritual at the Breakfast Table. *In* The American Dimension: Cultural Myths and Social Realities, W. Arens and Susan P. Montague, eds. Sherman Oaks, CA: Alfred Publishing Co., second edition. pp. 93-104.

Saraf, S.

1970 The Trichotomous Theme: a Ritual Category in Hindu Culture. Anthropos 65: 948-972.

Sarkar, Benoy Kumar

1914 The Positive Background of Hindu Sociology. Book I, Non-Political. Allahabad: The Panini Office.

Sharma, K. N.

[1961] Hindu Sects and Food Patterns in North India. *In* Aspects of Religion in Indian Society. L. P. Vidyarthi, editor. Meerut City: Kedar Nath Ram Nath. pp. 45-58.

Svertsen, Dagfinn

1963 When Caste Barriers Fall; a Study of Social and Economic Change in a South Indian Village. Norway: Universitets Forlaget.

Srinivas, M. N.

1952 Religion and Society among the Coorgs of South India. Bombay: Asia Publishing House.

1955 The Social System of a Mysore Village. *In* Village India, McKim Marriott, ed. Chicago: The University of Chicago Press. pp. 1-35.

1959 The Dominant Caste in Rampura. American Anthropologist 61:1: 1-16.

Srinivas, Tulasi

2006 'As Mother Made It': The Cosmopolitan Indian Family, 'Authentic' Food and the Construction of Cultural Utopia. International Journal of Sociology of the Family 32:2:191-221.

Stevenson, H. N. C.

1954 Status Evaluation in the Hindu Caste System. Journal of the Royal Anthropological Institute 84: 45-65.

Swaminathan, J., and R. K. Bhagavan

1966 Our Food. Madras: Ganesh and Co., Private Ltd.

Thurston, Edgar

1909 Tribes and Castes of Southern India. Madras: Government Press.

Turner, Victor

1966 The Syntax of Symbolism in an African Religion. Philosophical Transactions of the Royal Society, B, No. 772, Vol. 251, pp.295-304.

1967 The Forest of Symbols: Aspects of Ndembu Ritual. Ithaca: Cornell University Press.

Tyler, Stephen A.

1969 Context and Variation in Kaya Kinship Terminology. In Cognitive Anthropology. Stephen A. Tyler, editor. New York: Holt, Rinehart and Winston.

Underhill, Muriel Marion

1921 The Hindu Religious Year. London :Oxford University Press.

Vermeer, Donald E.

> 1970 Geophagy among the Ewe of Ghana. Ethnology 10: 56-72.

Walker, George B.

> 1968 The Hindu World: an Encyclopedic Survey of Hinduism. New York: Praeger.

Whitehead, Henry

> 1921 The Village Gods of South India. Calcutta: Association Press (Y.M.C.A.)

Wilson, H.H.

> 1958 Religious Sects of the Hindus. Calcutta: Susil Gupta (India) Private Ltd., second edition.

Wiser, Charlotte V.

> 1955 The Food of a Hindu Village of North India. Annals of the Missouri Botanical Garden 42: 301-412.

Yalman, Nur

> 1969 On the Meaning of Food Offerings in Ceylon. Forms of Symbolic Action. Proceedings of the 1969 Annual Spring Meeting of the American Ethnological Society, Robert F. Spencer, editor. Seattle and London: American Ethnological Society, distributed by the University of Washington Press. pp. 81-96.

INDEX

Made in the USA
Middletown, DE
21 April 2023